Politics in Commercial Society

Politics in Commercial Society

Jean-Jacques Rousseau and Adam Smith

~ ISTVAN HONT

edited by Béla Kapossy *and* Michael Sonenscher

Harvard University Press

Cambridge, Massachusetts
London, England
2015

First printing

*Library of Congress Cataloging-in-Publication Data is available
from the Library of Congress.*

ISBN 978-0-674-96770-0 (hardcover)

Contents

Acknowledgments

$\mathcal{P}$AUL SAGAR PROVIDED important help during the early phase of preparing this book for publication by comparing various electronic versions of the text, identifying and supplying references to quotations, and correcting numerous typos and grammatical errors. The editors would like to express their gratitude to him for his judicious contributions. Many thanks also to John Robertson, Richard Tuck, John Dunn, Keith Tribe, Isaac Nakhimovsky, Richard Whatmore, and Anna Hont for many helpful comments. Istvan Hont's friend and editor at Harvard University Press, Michael Aronson, encouraged the project from the outset and steered it through its various stages. Had Istvan Hont been allowed to see the publication of his Carlyle Lectures, he would have dedicated them to his wife, Anna. This book thus rightly belongs to her.

Editors' Introduction

ISTVAN HONT DIED in the spring of 2013, leaving a large number of unpublished works. The most wide ranging of these was also his last. This was the text of the six Carlyle Lectures on the thought of Adam Smith and Jean-Jacques Rousseau that he gave at Oxford University in the Hilary Term of 2009.[1] Hearing these lectures was intellectually exhilarating. Istvan Hont was a fine lecturer who did not need to prepare a detailed script to be able to talk fluently and precisely about the assortment of complicated subjects that he often addressed. But the care that he took to prepare these lectures for publication is both a sign of the significance that he attached to their content and an indication of the richness of the content itself. These are lectures that are best read, not heard, because they contain too much to absorb, even in six concentrated periods. They are the outcome—or distillation—of over thirty years of work, and it shows. They are, certainly, lectures about the thought of Adam Smith and Jean-Jacques Rousseau and, more specifically, about the real, though still largely unrecognized, analytical proximity of their respective theoretical concerns. But they are also, above all, lectures about modern politics—the politics of nation-states, global commerce, social inequality, international competitiveness,

---

1. The lectures were originally entitled "Visions of Politics in Commercial Society: Comparing Jean-Jacques Rousseau and Adam Smith." Hont drew on this text for the Schiller and the Benedict Lectures, which he gave in Jena and Boston, respectively, in 2010.

and, in a not entirely obvious sense, democratic accountability. These, as Hont put it in his final lecture, are the bread and butter of modern political theory. They were also, as he set out to show in these lectures, the subjects that gave rise to the surprisingly strong intellectual convergence between the thought of Rousseau and Smith.

The convergence itself was quite deliberate because it was actively generated by Smith. It is well known that Smith reviewed Rousseau's *Discourse on the Origin of Inequality* soon after it was published in 1755 and later recycled several key passages of his review in his *Theory of Moral Sentiments* of 1759. Although the fact is mentioned in the modern Glasgow edition of Smith's book, its still largely unexplored moral and political ramifications form much of the substance of Hont's lectures. As he shows in the first of them, Rousseau's examination of the feeling of pity and the oddly bifocal quality of its emotional orientation became the starting point of Smith's own, very subtle, moral theory. It has never been easy to identify and piece together the working parts of that theory, and Hont has taken a number of important steps to explain Smith's concept of an impartial spectator in ways that throw fresh light on the concept itself. One reason he was able to do so is that he had read Rousseau and Hobbes alongside Hutcheson and Hume and, by doing so, was able to position Smith's thought within the wider European intellectual context indicated by his initial review of Rousseau. In working out Smith's moral theory, Hont was also able to make full use of recent developments in Rousseau scholarship and, in particular, its reversion to eighteenth-century characterizations of Rousseau as a Hobbist or, at the least, a mitigated follower of seventeenth-century English political philosopher Thomas Hobbes.[2] This more historically and analytically accurate reading of Rousseau made it easier to see how Smith's treatment of the emotions could be positioned within a broader family of arguments about the self and its attributes that are now sometimes associated with late twentieth-century recognition theory.[3] From Hont's

2. This view was put forward notably by Richard Tuck, *The Rights of War and Peace: Political Thought and the International Order from Grotius to Kant* (Oxford: Oxford University Press, 1999), pp. 197–207; Béla Kapossy, *Iselin contra Rousseau: Sociable Patriotism and the History of Mankind* (Basel: Schwabe, 2006). See also Maurice Cranston and Richard S. Peters, eds., *Hobbes and Rousseau: A Collection of Critical Essays* (New York: Anchor Books, 1972).

3. Frederick Neuhouser, *Rousseau's Theodicy of Self-Love: Evil, Rationality, and the Drive for Recognition* (Oxford: Oxford University Press, 2008); Pierre Force, *Self-Interest before Adam Smith: A Genealogy of Economic Science* (Cambridge: Cambridge University Press,

perspective, recognition theory began with Hobbes, but it took Rousseau and Smith to work out fully what it implied for modern politics.

This shared interest in the self and its problematic character, particularly in the context of the mixture of dependence and independence formed by the division of labor and a commercial society, meant that Smith and Rousseau also shared the same set of intellectual interlocutors. One was the Anglo-Dutch political moralist Bernard Mandeville, whose discussion of pity in his *Fable of the Bees* gave much of the initial impetus to the Smith-Rousseau dialogue.[4] A second was the French magistrate Charles-Louis de Secondat, baron de Montesquieu, whose *The Spirit of Laws* (as the eighteenth-century English translation of the text was titled) provided almost all the subject matter (if not all the arguments) of the more extended version of the dialogue between Smith and Rousseau. A third, arguably more surprising, intellectual presence in the dialogue was that of the seventeenth-century English political theorist John Locke. Just as Hont's reconstruction of Smith's engagement with Rousseau in *The Theory of Moral Sentiments* makes it easier to see how Smith arrived at the concept of the impartial spectator, so too Hont's reconstruction of Rousseau's engagement with Locke makes it easier to see how Smith arrived at the unusual historical and political vision underlying the whole of *The Wealth of Nations*. For a long time it was usual to think that Rousseau and Smith were very different types of economic and political thinkers, with Smith said to be the great advocate of free trade, limited government, and a night-watchman state, whereas Rousseau was taken to be the eighteenth century's most famous critic of every aspect of the nexus of states and markets that, on Smith's terms, gave a commercial society its fundamental attributes. More recently, however, it has become more usual to point to their similarities, but to do so in ways that make Smith more like the old image of Rousseau, and both of them more like a certain type of modern, often American, political philosopher.[5] In these lectures, Hont has highlighted

2003). N. J. H. Dent and T. O'Hagan, "Rousseau on *Amour-Propre*," *Proceedings of the Aristotelian Society*, Supplement 72 (1998), pp. 57–74.

4. Edward Hundert, *The Enlightenment's Fable: Bernard Mandeville and the Discovery of Society* (Cambridge: Cambridge University Press, 1994); Mikko Tolonen, *Mandeville and Hume: Anatomists of Civil Society* (Oxford: Voltaire Foundation, 2013).

5. For initial indications of some of the problems, see Dennis C. Rasmussen, *The Problems and Promise of Commercial Society: Adam Smith's Response to Rousseau* (University Park: Pennsylvania State University Press, 2008), and the subsequent discussion between Rasmussen and Daniel B. Klein in *The Adam Smith Review* 7 (2013), pp. 323–31. See also Benjamin

the Smithian rather than the Rousseauian side of the comparison. In terms of the ancient nomenclatures often given to the eighteenth-century moral and political typologies underlying Hont's interpretation, both Rousseau and Smith were Epicureans.[6]

This convergence is the basis of the not entirely facetious titles of the first two chapters. It is well known that there was once said to be an "Adam Smith Problem," or the problem that arose when comparing the putatively altruistic moral theory of *The Theory of Moral Sentiments* to the more blatantly selfish theory of *The Wealth of Nations*. The same type of problem, according to Hont, applies to Rousseau. In this case, it is not easy to see how Rousseau's bleak account of the dynamics of recognition seeking, property formation, and class differentiation in his *Discourse on the Origin of Inequality* (referred to as the second *Discourse*) can be reconciled with the idea of a social contract and a sovereign general will that formed the analytical core of *The Social Contract*. There was, in short, a "Jean-Jacques Rousseau Problem," as the German philosopher Ernst Cassirer put it in a public lecture in 1932, echoing the nineteenth-century German historical economist August Oncken's earlier, and now better-known, announcement of the Adam Smith

Fridén, *Rousseau's Economic Philosophy: Beyond the Market of Innocents* (Dordrecht: Kluwer Academic Publishers, 1998); Samuel Fleischacker, *On Adam Smith's "Wealth of Nations": A Philosophical Companion* (Princeton, NJ: Princeton University Press, 2004); Catherine Larrère, "Adam Smith et Jean-Jacques Rousseau: sympathie et pitié," in *Kairos* 20 (2002), pp. 73–94; Emma Rothschild, *Economic Sentiments: Adam Smith, Condorcet, and the Enlightenment* (Cambridge, MA: Harvard University Press, 2001). For helpful ways into the broader literature on Smith, see Knud Haakonssen, ed., *The Cambridge Companion to Adam Smith* (Cambridge: Cambridge University Press, 2006); Knud Haakonssen, ed., *Adam Smith* (Aldershot: Ashgate, 1998); Christopher L. Berry, Maria Pia Paganelli, and Craig Smith, eds., *The Oxford Handbook of Adam Smith* (Oxford: Oxford University Press, 2013). See also the following annual publications: *The Adam Smith Review*, 7 vols. to date (London: Routledge, 2004–2013), and the *Annales de la Société Jean-Jacques Rousseau*, 51 vols. to date (Geneva: Droz, 1905–2013).

6. Hont first presented his comparative study of Smith's and Rousseau's moral theory at a conference (Grotius and the Stoa) in Gorinchem in 2001. For recent studies, see Fonna Forman-Barzilai, *Adam Smith and the Circles of Sympathy* (Cambridge: Cambridge University Press, 2010); Michael Frazer, *The Enlightenment of Sympathy: Justice and the Moral Sentiments in the Eighteenth Century and Today* (Oxford: Oxford University Press, 2010); Jerry Evensky, *Adam Smith's Moral Philosophy: A Historical and Contemporary Perspective on Markets, Law, Ethics, and Culture* (Cambridge: Cambridge University Press, 2005). For Hont's account of Rousseau as a Cynic, see Michael Sonenscher, *Sans-Culottes: An Eighteenth-Century Emblem in the French Revolution* (Princeton, NJ: Princeton University Press, 2008).

Problem.[7] Hont's initial juxtaposition of the two problems makes it easier not only to get the measure of each but also to see more of the content and shape of their respective outcomes.

As the sequence of lectures was intended to emphasize, the Jean-Jacques Rousseau Problem came first. It did so not only because Rousseau's early publications preceded *The Theory of Moral Sentiments* but also because, as Smith's initial assessment of Rousseau already showed, the genealogy of human emotions that Rousseau began to present in his second *Discourse* (and which continued in what Hont has called Rousseau's "third discourse," meaning his *Essay on the Origin of Languages*) gave Smith the analytical means to move beyond the antagonistic positions in moral and political philosophy held by his two most important intellectual interlocutors, Francis Hutcheson and David Hume. Behind Hutcheson and Hume lay the thought of Bernard Mandeville, and as Hont, echoing Smith, shows, it was Rousseau's treatment of Mandeville that appeared to offer a way to take the related subjects of sociability, morality, and politics to a higher level of analytical sophistication than was currently available in a purely Anglophone context.

The main title of the first two chapters, "Commercial Sociability," is a compound of two eighteenth-century terms. (Hont, it is worth noting, had an unusual talent for putting words together to draw out their respective conceptual significance.) The "commercial" part of the phrase was intended to echo Smith's term, "commercial society." The "sociability" part, on the other hand, alluded to a huge body of largely theological, natural jurisprudential, or what would now be called anthropological, discussions of human nature in the seventeenth and eighteenth centuries. At one time, putting the two terms together to form the phrase "commercial sociability" would have been seen as a tautology. By the mid-eighteenth century, however, it was just as likely to have been seen as an oxymoron. In the first sense, the word "commerce" was almost a synonym of "society." In the second sense, however, it was more like its antonym. As Hont went to some lengths to show, the deep-seated tension between these two meanings of the phrase helps explain why,

---

7. August Oncken, "Das Adam Smith-Problem," in *Zeitschrift für Sozialwissenschaft*, ed. Julius Wolf, vol. 1 (Berlin: G. Reimer, 1898), pp. 25–33, 101–8, 267–87; Ernst Cassirer, "Das Problem Jean Jacques Rousseau," *Archiv für Geschichte der Philosophie* 41 (1933), pp. 479–513. For an English-language version, see Ernst Cassirer, *The Question of Jean-Jacques Rousseau*, ed. and trans. Peter Gay (New York: Columbia University Press, 1954).

notwithstanding Albert Hirschman's classic study, considerably more than a switch from the passions to the interests was—and still is—required to make sense of the moral and political dimensions of what Smith was the first to call a commercial (as opposed to a hunting, pastoral, or agricultural) society.[8] Hont went on to show that the two parts of the phrase were subsequently given the names *Gemeinschaft* and *Gesellschaft* by the great nineteenth-century Hobbes scholar Ferdinand Tönnies.[9] This linguistic fusion of opposites is both a helpful indication of the real moral and political problems involved in the concept of a commercial society and, Hont argued, a warning that, despite the apparently outdated appearance of the phrases, there might have really been a Jean-Jacques Rousseau Problem and an Adam Smith Problem. As Hont implied, it is not clear whether either has actually been laid to rest by modern political theory.

The similarity between the two labels and the conceptual overlap between the Rousseau problem and the Smith problem was one reason for Hont's abiding interest in Immanuel Kant's term "unsocial sociability," not only because it helped to capture much of the problematic character of the concept of commercial sociability but also because it pointed toward what, beginning in the last two decades of the eighteenth century, began to happen intellectually once it became possible to think about Rousseau and Smith together, as Kant undoubtedly did. In this sense, Hont's treatment of the Rousseau-Smith dialogue was part of his broader concern with thinking about politics, mainly between the time of Thomas Hobbes on the one side and Karl Marx on the other, and mainly in light of what was involved—historically as well as analytically—in thinking about politics and economics together. In this framework, modern political theory had as much to do with the reaction to Hobbes as with Hobbes's thought itself, making Rousseau and Smith heirs to both, notably where Hobbes's legacy resurfaced in the thought of Samuel Pufendorf and John Locke. The broader temporal and analytical perspective that Hont brought to bear on the Smith-Rousseau relationship was the starting point of the second pair of his lectures, namely those dealing with governments and their histo-

8. Albert O. Hirschman, *The Passions and the Interests: Political Arguments for Capitalism before Its Triumph* (Princeton, NJ: Princeton University Press, 1977).

9. Ferdinand Tönnies, *Gemeinschaft und Gesellschaft: Abhandlung des Kommunismus und des Sozialismus als empirischen Kulturformen* (Leipzig: Fues's Verlag, 1887).

ries and, more specifically, with the relationship between Europe's two histories, one ancient and largely southern in origin; the other modern and mainly northern in origin.

Hont was acutely conscious of the tension between the normative and the historical in the history of political thought. One reason for his abiding hostility to the idea that there had ever been such a thing as a "Cambridge School" of the history of political thought was that it was hard to identify anything like a consistent (or possibly even a considered) range of responses to that tension among the hypothetical school's putative members. Hont's own way of dealing with the tension can be seen at its best in the two chapters on governments and their histories, which follow his examination of the problem of commercial sociability in Rousseau and Smith. Here he went to some lengths to identify and describe the connections between what still seem to be two distinct approaches to the history and historiography of political thought. The first has a more obviously normative dimension because of its focus on rights and its association with the natural jurisprudence of Hugo Grotius, Thomas Hobbes, Samuel Pufendorf, and John Locke. The second has an equally obvious historical dimension because of its focus on republics and on the various moral, economic, or political arrangements involved in what have variously come to be called civic humanism, neo-Roman liberty, or simply republicanism. By using Rousseau and Smith as guides to the conceptual components of these two historiographical traditions, Hont was able not only to show how much conceptual common ground they once shared but also to explain why the subject of government and its origins lay at the heart of the tension between the normative and the historical that has become so prominent a feature of the history and historiography of political thought.

Here, Hont's long familiarity with the thought of David Hume helped to make it easier to see what united—and what divided—Rousseau and Smith. In thinking about how to escape from the slide toward property, inequality, and ultimately revolution, Rousseau relied heavily on the political thought of John Locke and, more particularly, on the resistance theory built into Locke's argument in his *Two Treatises of Government* against the patriarchal political theory of Sir Robert Filmer. As Hont shows, Rousseau's description of the political arrangements that existed prior to the establishment of a fully contractual political association was similar to Locke's account of the state of nature in his second

Treatise. First, there was a rudimentary society that came to be divided by property, money, and inequality; then, there was a social contract and a government; finally, and in light of the initial misbehavior of the government, there was a constitution and a constitutional government. Rousseau followed this sequence. On his terms, the law came first, and government followed. Smith, however, followed the opposite sequence. Government came first, with the law and legislation following.[10] As Hont shows, this difference owed a great deal to the thought of David Hume, particularly to Hume's account of property formation and his parallel examination of justice as an artificial virtue. It meant, as Hont also shows, that the real republican, at least in terms of the stylized typologies of the recent history and historiography of political thought, was not Rousseau but Smith. Hume's legacy meant that of the two, it was Smith who was best placed to follow the logic of the seventeenth-century English political thinker James Harrington's assertion that the balance of political power followed the balance of property and who, as a result, was also best equipped to explain why modern politics were different from ancient politics. On Hont's terms, it is not entirely clear that Harrington's political thought was as ancient and Machiavellian in its evaluative orientation as it is now usually taken to be. Seen through the prism of Hume's and Smith's respective historical and political visions, Harrington's political thought had as much to do with the hazards as with the promise of reviving ancient politics in a modern setting.

Montesquieu and Hume had pointed the way, but it was Smith, more than Rousseau, who developed the most elaborate account of the gulf that had opened up between the ancients and the moderns. The centerpiece of this account was the idea that Europe had a double history, made up of two historical cycles: the first southern and Roman, and the second northern and German—in both content and consequences. This double history, Hont argued, was the basis of Smith's claim, set out most fully in Book 3 of *The Wealth of Nations*, that the "unnatural and retrograde order" underlying the history of modern European political so-

10. Hont first developed this argument in detail in a lecture given at the University of Chicago in 1989, "From Economics to Politics and Back: The Origins of Private Property, Inequality and the State, and Adam Smith's Two Versions of the Four Stages Theory." It was developed much further in Hont, "Adam Smith's History of Law and Government as Political Theory," in *Political Judgement: Essays for John Dunn*, ed. Richard Bourke and Raymond Geuss (Cambridge: Cambridge University Press, 2009), pp. 131–71.

cieties (meaning the way that urban society and manufacturing industry had developed ahead of rural society and agriculture) contained enough of a mixture of both the ancient and the modern to forestall or obstruct a replay of the cycle of decline and fall that had brought Europe's first, Rome-driven history to an end. This way of thinking about what had come out of the decline and fall of the Roman Empire began with Montesquieu's analysis of the feudal afterlife of the Germanic invasions of imperial Rome.[11] As Hont proceeded to show, Smith's version of this history—with its emphasis first on the moral and political legacies of the structures of authority and power prevailing in the shepherd societies that overran the Roman Empire, and then on the concentrations of industry and trade that developed in the fortified towns that survived after Rome's decline and fall—was the basis of what, some two centuries later, came to be known as the Whig interpretation of history. In other, more elaborate guises, however, it was also the starting point of the many philosophies of history of the nineteenth century, stretching from Hegel and Comte to Tocqueville, Mill, Marx, and Weber.

The final two chapters of the book go a long way toward establishing some of the connections between the thought of Rousseau and Smith and these later developments in the history of nineteenth-century political thought. As Hont presented them, Rousseau and Smith not only shared the same intellectual ground but also shared the same intellectual failure. They did so, Hont suggests, because in the last analysis, it is still not clear what type of politics best fits a commercial society. This is not only because the concept of a commercial society is not fully self-explanatory but also, and more brutally, because the world as it is contains considerably more than one commercial society, with the result that thinking about politics and commercial society calls for thinking about their external as well as their internal dynamics. Here, as Hont shows, there was a real divergence between Rousseau and Smith. Although both acknowledged that modern societies were commercial societies, they differed in their conceptions of what the political economy of a commercial society had to be. With Rousseau, the emphasis fell on self-sufficiency, not only in terms of economic resources but also, and more importantly, in terms of the relationship between individual

---

11. Michael Sonenscher, *Before the Deluge: Public Debt, Inequality, and the Intellectual Origins of the French Revolution* (Princeton, NJ: Princeton University Press, 2007).

households and the state, or between the private and the public. With Smith, the emphasis fell more on the side of productivity, again not only in terms of economic resources but also in terms of the scale and scope of state institutions and their institutional life. Here too, however, it is easy to exaggerate the divergences. If Rousseau's intellectual and po-litical posterity included the French theorist of the representative system Emmanuel-Joseph Sieyès and the German philosopher Georg Wilhelm Friedrich Hegel, while Smith's intellectual legacy was adopted most fully by, for example, the French political economist Jean-Baptiste Say and his Swiss contemporary Benjamin Constant, it is not particularly clear how far apart these pairs actually were.

Modern states are usually fiscal states; in addition, they are often wel-fare states and sometimes federal states too. Much of the point of Hont's original six lectures was to encourage his listeners to think about Rous-seau and Smith in light of these labels and the tensions between the different types of resources, entitlements, and obligations that they indi-cate. Istvan Hont spent most of his academic career as a member of the history faculty of the University of Cambridge. Yet he thought of him-self first and foremost as a political theorist, although not of the formal or analytical kind. He was convinced of the need to study contempo-rary politics and intellectual history together, and was persuaded that modern political theory could move forward only by paying careful at-tention to the ideas of the best commentators on past instances of modern society. To him, Smith and Rousseau, together with Hume and Kant, belonged to that category. Thus, reconstructing the political thought of Rousseau and Smith, or that of any other thinker for that matter, had to be more than purely historical. To Hont, the historical insights mattered not only because comparisons are a helpful way to make sense of the work of any particular individual but also because the time-bound character of the conceptual side of politics means that a great deal is likely to be lost without the combination of historical knowledge and historical sensitivity that is on display in these lectures. Anyone wanting to find out what the concepts of sociability or political economy once meant, or trying to describe the Enlightenment, or seeking to under-stand what was involved in describing someone as a Stoic, a Cynic, or an Epicurean in the eighteenth century, or wondering why calling someone an optimist in the eighteenth century was rather like calling someone a realist now will learn more than he or she might have expected from reading these lectures. The same, of course, applies to Jean-Jacques Rousseau and Adam Smith and the many ways that their surprisingly detailed dialogue came to structure the debates of subsequent generations of thinkers. As Istvan Hont showed, the two sets of subjects are closer than they seem.

A Note on the Text

$\mathcal{A}$s with most of his projects, Istvan Hont hoped to develop his Carlyle Lectures into a larger study, which would have included a comparative study of Kant and, if the Cambridge graduate seminar course he prepared for the Easter Term 2012 (Rousseau, Smith, Marx) is anything to go by, also of Marx. As it is, these lectures form a coherent and highly structured study that needs no further elaboration. Istvan Hont left various electronic copies of his lectures, of which the most recent has been used as the basis for the text printed here. The editors have tried to keep as much as possible of Hont's distinctive style and have limited editorial interventions to a minimum. This has, however, included correcting obvious errors and rephrasing certain expressions or sentences that seemed insufficiently clear. All references to primary sources were added during the process of editing. References to secondary literature, apart from references to Hont's own work, have been added only when that literature has been mentioned in the text.

∾ 1

Commercial Sociability: The Jean-Jacques Rousseau Problem

𝒯HIS BOOK IS ABOUT commercial society and how to understand politics in it. It will attempt to tease apart the different sorts of political vision that are currently relevant to us by using the history of political thought as a guide. It takes a pair of thinkers who are usually contrasted rather than likened to each other because one is undoubtedly a republican whereas the other is usually seen as not. How similar or different their politics were is what we shall see. My aim, at least rhetorically, is to produce parallels and contrasts that are surprising. It is not unusual to contrast Rousseau and Smith, with the former seen as an enemy of, and the latter as an apologist for, modernity. To repeat this outcome, even in a more sophisticated form, wouldn't be very interesting. Rather, the attempt here is to learn from the revisionist historiography of political thought of the last thirty years. Our pictures of both Rousseau and Smith have changed, or at least they ought to have changed. Now, what happens if we take these new views of Rousseau and Smith and juxtapose them? Perhaps new aspects, fresh views, of their thought will come into focus and we can gain more in our understanding of their work. The view from Cambridge is that the new historiography of political thought has become stale and needs a push forward. John Pocock, who used to work on the seventeenth century and now works on the eighteenth, has complained about the Cambridge

1

fixation with the seventeenth century. The chapters that follow are designed to help this leap forward.

The main title of the first two of these chapters indicates that Rousseau and Smith shared a view of the type of society whose politics they wanted to change. The subtitles of these particular chapters also indicate that there might well be a "Jean-Jacques Rousseau problem" as well as an "Adam Smith problem," and that there is a tension and maybe even a paradox hidden in the assumption that there is a common denominator underlying the ideas of the Genevan and the Scotsman (emphatically, we must not call them a Frenchman and an Englishman). I claim that many of Smith's ideas were much closer to Rousseau's than is commonly thought. In addition, I advance a seemingly radical argument: I will argue that both Rousseau and Smith—not only Smith, as is conventionally argued—were theorists of commercial society. It is their theoretical proximity, at least on some key issues, that makes them proper and interesting subjects of comparative study. Rousseau as a theorist of commercial society? This sounds paradoxical, at least from the point of view of our standard understanding of Rousseau. Of course, the suggestion here is precisely that the common view of Rousseau might be seriously inadequate.

I am a Smith scholar, and my interpretation is driven by my long-standing struggle to understand him. Nonetheless, in this book, Rousseau is not simply a foil. Their work intersected, not through personal acquaintance but academically, through Smith's reading of Rousseau. He reviewed Rousseau, and there is every reason to assume that this review offers an important key to a possible new reading of both Rousseau and Smith. I will get to an account of this review by the end of the chapter. My main task till then is to prepare you for it.

There is already something called "Das Adam Smith Problem," pointing to a difficulty with the view that Smith was a genuine moral theorist of commercial society. I will briefly analyze this issue at the end of this chapter. At this moment, it should suffice to say that I want to extend this reading of Smith and assimilate Rousseau to it, to make it a case of two intertwined problems, "Das Adam Smith Problem" and the analogous "Das Jean-Jacques Rousseau Problem." I hope that this will illuminate the ideas of both thinkers significantly. The pivot on which this pairing turns is the notion of commercial society. Once it is factored into our understanding of the two philosophers, it may make some of their ideas look paradoxical. This chapter is an introduction to this apparently perverse approach. I ask the following questions: How does the concept of commercial society serve as a fundamental term for comparing Rousseau and Smith? What *is* commercial society? What is its meaning and history as a concept?

One must admit, from the outset, that despite its current ubiquity in the historiography of political thought, "commercial society" is not a term that is readily understood or widely used. There is perhaps a clear notion or concept underlying it, but in modern usage, the term is not unambiguous. "Commercial society" is Smith's own term; perhaps nobody else used it in quite the same linguistic fashion, even if strong theoretical affinities with his usage did exist. It is Smith's own use of this expression that validates it historically, but this validation is not outstandingly strong. It is just barely there.

Normally, "commercial society" refers to a society of traders or of market economic agents in general, describing a society in which there is much commercial activity. It was this quite ordinary, if not terribly common, meaning that Smith stretched further in order to make it a theoretical object for moral and political inquiry—as a fundamental type of society. He also used the term to describe a kind of society in which, quantitatively, there was a great deal of commercial and market activity. The quantitative increase of commercial or commercial-type transactions in a society was for Smith an important index of social change. As we shall see in his account of the Greek polis, he used the presence of a quantitative increase of transactional activity in a society as an index of qualitative changes in the basic modus operandi of that society. He then stretched the term to describe a society whose members related to one another as interactive commercial individuals, behaving generally as merchants act when entering a market. What Smith wished to say was that their social relations within their own society became market-like, governed by the utility that such market liaisons both demand and entail.

The issue was not whether the members of such a society traded a great deal with one another but whether they related within such societies as traders. A commercial society is first of all constituted commercially on the inside, rather than through its external activities. The concept of commercial society describes the constitutive moral quality of the membership of this society, not the actual material trading activity itself. Traditionally, Christians heavily criticized commercial society. A partnership of Christian traders might be designated as a commercial association or trading society in the conventional sense. But their external trading activities wouldn't necessarily turn their group into a commercial society in Smith's sense. Theirs could remain a society of Christian fellowship, with large doses (at least in theory) of beneficence, friendship, and solidarity to glue it together. However, once they started to behave toward one another as traders, as market agents rather than as Christian brothers, they would become a commercial society in the full Smithian sense.

Commercial or market society is obviously a fundamental type of society, which we should readily be able to comprehend under this name. Alas, we often cannot. Although today the term "commercial society" is fashionable in scholarship, it is more often than not used incorrectly and in a theoretically imprecise sense. In fact, as a theoretical category, *commercial society* is hardly used correctly at all. This kind of problem is, of course, a general feature of political discourse. Most of its central categories have no properly designated and accepted names. We speak and write by using many ambiguous and confused descriptors. It is perhaps sufficient to mention the fundamental ambiguity surrounding the term "state." In fact, the issue of commercial society is a particularly important component of the answer to the question, what is the modern state? The phrase "politics in commercial society," given to the title of this book, refers to the problems involved in identifying the kind of state that might best complement a commercial society.

This difficulty of naming our central political categories is not a new problem, although one might have expected some progress in the wake of recent developments in historical contextualism. Experience shows that contextualism helps in identifying particular idioms of speech within historical political discourse, but it is less productive when naming key concepts that transcend linguistic fashion. Think about the notorious problems involved in identifying the meaning of terms like "republics" or "republicanism," or of particular types of liberty. The ambiguity of naming political phenomena and concepts is not simply a problem for historians; it is deeply embedded in the historical subject matter itself (just think about the untranslatability of such key terms as the Greek polis and the Latin *civitas*) and it often persists over a very long time.

The phrase "commercial society" first emerged in the context of eighteenth-century political language. What would be a later category that captures its sense most productively? Perhaps the best-known modern signposting is the *Gesellschaft* and *Gemeinschaft* distinction of the German sociologist Ferdinand Tönnies, originating from 1887, from which the modern American political language of communitarianism has developed.[1] Importantly, Tönnies was a historian of political thought. He was a Hobbes scholar, and his categories were fundamentally translations of terms prevalent in Hobbes's *Elements of Law: Natural and Political* (a text that Tönnies edited) and his *De Cive*. Knowing this fact restores some historical sense to Tönnies's categories, for it allows us to see that instead of regarding Smith and Rousseau as having anticipated Tönnies, as is usually stated, Tönnies was in fact adapting even older categories of political language to modern usage. This eliminates prolepsis, the one sin on whose rejection the Cambridge School unanimously agrees, at least in theory if not always in practice. Some historians of political thought find it depressing that one can never get away from Hobbes in the history of English-speaking political thought, but in the case of the *Gesellschaft–Gemeinschaft* distinction, such a regress, if that is what it is (fortunately it isn't an infinite regress), is historically justified.

Sometimes Hegel, rather than Tönnies, is mentioned in the context of the genealogy of the concept of commercial society. The precise meaning of his term "civil society" is too complicated to discuss here, but suffice it to say that Hegel's civil society, or *bürgerliche Gesellschaft*, was the standard European vernacular rendition of the Latin term *civitas*, the very same term that Hobbes used as his baseline for his theory of the state. Often *civitas* was also translated as "state," and Hegel's argument was about the definition of the state or, more precisely, the people's state, *Volksstaat*, which was to some degree innovative. For Hegel, the state was a Christian and post-Roman term. It was meant to signal more than a Roman state because it was to be understood as a modern synthesis of the Greek polis and the Roman *civitas* together, glued together with an application of Christian Trinitarianism. The other name of the state, civil society, signified a component or the infrastructure of the

---

1. Ferdinand Tönnies, *Gemeinschaft und Gesellschaft: Abhandlung des Communismus und des Socialismus als empirischen Culturformen* (Leipzig: Fues's Verlag, 1887).

state. It described the heritage of the Roman *civitas* as modified for a non-slave-owning market society.

The idea that there must exist an appropriate modern terminology for commercial society that could serve as a vehicle for a comparative study of Rousseau and Smith (and potentially of many others) is simply an illusion. Most scholars use terms like "commercial society" to get away from Marxist language and the categories of sociology. Terms like "capitalism," "bourgeois society," and "inorganic society" now seem to be both loaded and disturbingly sloppy as categories. Adopting the term "commercial society" was a well-intentioned departure from this vocabulary. It is, however, an unfinished journey, and one purpose of this chapter is to throw some light on its possible use in political thought. In the next section, I intend to pursue this hunt for categories and concepts just a little bit further, in order to uncover layers of language that allow us to gain more fruitful access to our texts.

It is well recognized in the literature that Tönnies's notion of *Gesellschaft* is directly indebted to Hobbes's notion of the state. In contrast, there is a general assumption that *Gemeinschaft* is drawn from Romantic sources, subsequently spruced up by late nineteenth-century anthropology and sociology. This is not correct. Both concepts were derived from Hobbes. This has not been easily recognizable because the original Hobbesian terminology is all but forgotten. The Hobbesian pair of concepts were "union" and "concord." These fundamental categories, which loom large in *De Cive*, became submerged in *Leviathan*, which focused exclusively on union. Tönnies knew his *Leviathan* well. He was, however, also the most important modern editor of *The Elements of Law*. It is in *The Elements of Law* and *De Cive* that the terminology of union and concord was prominent.

Union, not concord, was the primary concept of *Leviathan*. It was the root idea underlying Hobbes's theory of the state by representation. In Tönnies, the *Gesellschaft–Gemeinschaft* distinction appears as "sociological," as a differentiation between two concepts of society. In Hobbes, it was intensely political. The concord–union distinction was *the* central plank of Hobbes's attack on republicanism and resistance theory. In *De Cive*, Hobbes attempted to erase the influence of the Aristotelian tradition by expressly denying that man was a naturally social being, because he wished to destroy the idea that naturally sociable beings could also be naturally political. He denied the political efficacy of natural sociability as the foundation of the state in any of its forms, including the utilitarian bonds created by commercial reciprocity. Instead, he constructed a theory of indirect popular sovereignty that offered stability and peace without any preexisting consensus or prepolitical social integration. On its basis, Hobbes claimed for himself the title of the founder of modern political science. He described his commonwealth or state as a "union." The alternative model, which required preexisting consensus and hence a grounding in sociability, Hobbes called "concord." This formal division of the types of commonwealths into two was built on preexisting distinctions, but his insistence on drawing a very sharp dividing line between them as separate forms of community and his presentation of a new explanation of the genesis of union were genuine innovations.

It seems that Hobbes dismissed commercial sociability as ultimately irrelevant to his political purposes. In *De Cive*, he declared that a lasting polity anchored to a "concord" or "consensus" of citizens was a forlorn hope. Only a "union," the *Gegenbegriff* (counterconcept) of "concord," could be the foundation of a modern state. A union, Hobbes claimed, created political unity by representation, assuming no more than an absolute minimum of consensus based on fear for one's life and the desire for self-preservation. Hobbes rejected Aristotle's notion that man was a political or social animal, a *zoon politikon*, to pull the rug from under the idea of a sociable commonwealth.

Hobbes therefore dismissed the notion of man's innate sociability. Had "man naturally loved his fellow man" he argued, there would be a global society of all. But instead of a society of mankind we have a multiplicity of separate nations and states. The purpose of political theory, Hobbes claimed, was to explain the practices of these distinct national societies that were grounded not in the "love of all" but in the "love of self." For the effective operation of the state, Hobbes argued, "friendship" was secondary. Although he denied that love had been an effective force in human life, Hobbes acknowledged that utility was a genuine cause of society. Although underplayed in his system, he had a perfectly serviceable theory of acquired commercial sociability.[2]

When Hobbes claimed that man was not a *zoon politikon*, he claimed that humans lacked the qualities of higher sociability that can serve as the foundation of politics. Hobbes's innovation was to offer a vision of

2. Thomas Hobbes, *De Cive: The Latin Version*, ed. H. Warrander (Oxford: Oxford University Press, 1984), 1.2.

politics that operated without preexisting concord or consensus as a foundation of the state. Today, one would refer in this context to Aristotle's idea of friendship as an opposite model of sociability—one that creates a polis—but this argument was not brought up directly by Smith or Rousseau in this context, although Aristotle's distinctions did not go unnoticed. It is interesting to note, however, that Smith deals with the issue of friendship and the construction of commercial society side by side in *The Theory of Moral Sentiments*.

For Hobbes, if there is no sociability, no concord of a primary or fundamental kind is possible. The word "concord" appears often in *Leviathan* as part of the couplet "peace and concord," describing the aim of the new kind of state. This hides the meaning of *concord* given in the *Elements* and *De Cive* rather than showcases it. Concord, of course, is also the aim of union, a consequence of it. Concord, consensus, is necessary for states.

The problem here is one of sequencing—that is, whether concord precedes the formation of a political regime or is the consequence of it (this is a well-known problem in nationalism theories, in which blood or racial relations guarantee pre-state—as well as post-state—concord). The concord of *Leviathan* is secondary, post-state concord. The issue was the existence of pre-state concord or of an alternative concord to the one created by Hobbes's state. Returning to Tönnies for the last time, it is important to notice that he describes *Gemeinschaft* as a social unit of concord. In this sense, Tönnies points us toward the idea that the unstated third person in any Rousseau-Smith comparison is Hobbes. Although this is interesting in itself, tracing Tönnies back to Hobbes is only interesting for us here if there was a genuine historical connection backing it up. Fortunately, such a connection exists. Smith brought up the notion of commercial society in a context that is directly related to a Hobbesian genealogy.

Commercial society for Smith is a model of a lower-order secondary concord, an addition or alternative to Hobbes's model of secondary concord created by union. Smith talks about commercial society twice directly and importantly, once in *The Theory of Moral Sentiments* and once in *The Wealth of Nations*. *The Theory of Moral Sentiments* reference is more important, because the context is directly related to Hobbes and is outside the framework of talking about issues of commerce and political economy in any direct and obvious manner. In this work, Smith's discussion of commercial society is part of a discussion of moral theory.

In *The Theory of Moral Sentiments*, Smith repeats the concord–union distinction without using these terms, and then inserts a third, intermediate term in between. It is less than concord but more than the state of complete lack of sociability that is the underlying precondition of the concept of union. In this work, Smith outlines three forms of society: that of love, fear, and utility.

1. Where the necessary assistance is reciprocally afforded from love, from gratitude, from friendship, and esteem, the society flourishes and is happy. All the different members of it are bound together by the agreeable bands of love and affection, and are, as it were, drawn to one common centre of mutual good offices.[3]

2. Society, however, cannot subsist among those who are at all times ready to hurt and injure one another. The moment that injury begins, the moment that mutual resentment and animosity take place, all the bands of it are broke asunder, and the different members of which it consisted are, as it were, dissipated and scattered abroad by the violence and opposition of their discordant affections. If there is any society among robbers and murderers, they must at least, according to the trite observation, abstain from robbing and murdering one another. Beneficence, therefore, is less essential to the existence of society than justice.[4]

Smith positioned the third model, commercial society, between these two extremes, although in an asymmetrical fashion. He claimed that society can subsist, though not in the most comfortable state, without beneficence; but the prevalence of injustice must utterly destroy it. This not very comfortable society was commercial society:

3. Society may subsist among different men, as among different merchants, from a sense of its utility, without any mutual love or affection; and though no man in it should owe any obligation, or be bound in gratitude to any other, it may still be upheld by a mercenary exchange of good offices according to an agreed valuation.[5]

---

3. Adam Smith, *The Theory of Moral Sentiments*, in *The Glasgow Edition of the Works and Correspondence of Adam Smith* [hereafter *TMS*], ed. D. D. Raphael and A. L. Macfie (Oxford: Oxford University Press, 1976), II.ii.3.1.

4. Ibid., II.ii.3.3.

5. Ibid., II.ii.3.2.

In *The Wealth of Nations*, Smith names this entity as commercial society.[6]

At this point, it is worth asking whether anybody else had a term for utility-based sociability and, if so, what had happened to it? Why did it disappear, if indeed it did, from people's perception of Hobbes's political theory? It is worth asking this question because Hobbes's emphasis on his strategically most important aims led to the assumption that he didn't understand or appreciate other idioms; thus, his remarks on less prominent but still important subjects, as in this case of sociability, have been mostly unnoticed and certainly underappreciated.

Friendship, meaning high sociability that is able to create a political culture of true concord or—inversely—even the dismissal of it, was not the most contentious issue raised by Hobbes's move. The most often cited notion of sociability was that societies are held together by need. Although this claim about need as the cause of society and as the basis of the specificity of the polis was often associated with Aristotle, it did not in fact originate in Aristotle. Here, reference was often made in this context both to Plato's *Republic* and to Aristotle's description of the network of households and foreign trade. Hobbes certainly did play down the idea that society is created by mutual need and also registered the complaints arising from this omission. He answered them in one of those long footnotes in the second edition of *De Cive* (1647) that were designed to be replies to his critics. Like Pufendorf a little later, Hobbes accepted that need *(indigentia)* was a powerful cause of society *(societas)* because it was a facilitator of the human pursuit of profit *(utile)* and advantage *(commodium)*. Need gave rise to steady social agency, even if it was nothing like friendship or love. When critics of the early version of *De Cive* objected to Hobbes's dismissal of utilitarian sociability, he answered that he was not "denying that we seek each other's company *(congressus)* at the prompting of nature *(nature cogente appetere)*" and did not deny that men (even nature compelling) desire to come together *(alteru, alterus congressum)*.[7] Humans were social rather than solitary creatures. Being in dire need was a genuine evil. Had they lived alone, children could not survive and adults could not "live well." The time-honored

6. Adam Smith, *An Inquiry into the Nature and Causes of the Wealth of Nations*, in *The Glasgow Edition of the Works and Correspondence of Adam Smith*, ed. R. H. Campbell, A. S. Skinner, and W. B. Todd (Oxford: Oxford University Press, 1976), I.iv.1.

7. Hobbes, *De Cive*, 1.2 annotation.

comparison between animal and human societies was correct. Humans were weak and lacked the terrifying natural weapons of brutes (horns, teeth, and stings; Kant used the very same argument later for establishing his "unsocial sociability"). Animal needs, however, were limited and fixed, whereas humans, though physically weak, had other abilities. Eventually, society enabled men to acquire artificial weapons (swords and guns) that eclipsed anything to be found among animals. Hobbes enthusiastically praised the arts and the sciences as the causes of "the enormous advantages of human life," which "far surpassed the life of animals." He claimed that it was language—the communicative medium of sociability—that made humans so vastly superior to animals. Language led to numeracy, which led to the sciences, which resulted in high material civilization.[8] Both Rousseau and Smith repeated this very same move, which we must take note of for later analysis.

To sum up. Hobbes acknowledged that physical need was an important cause of society through utility. However, he emphasized that there was another need in humans that also caused society: their need for recognition by others. This was a psychological need, as strong and as original as physical need. The urge to seek recognition was strong and was impossible to satisfy without creating society. However, Hobbes emphasized, it was a strongly disruptive need. Recognition expressed itself as a desire for superiority, and as such, it was a zero-sum game, resulting in winners and losers. Thus, utilitarian economic sociability could be additive, while the psychological need for recognition could not, except through strict equality in recognition—a possibility Hobbes denied. As Hobbes claimed, the dynamics of psychological need were bound to overwhelm the dynamics of physical neediness, and it was the first, not the second, that was foundational for understanding politics.

In the Hobbesian picture, strong sociability, which could cause concord, is dismissed. What remains is a struggle, an antagonism, a tension—call it what you will—between utility and pride, wherein Hobbes claims that understanding politics must involve an analysis of pride, glory seeking or vainglory seeking. In other words, he claimed that understanding politics stems from the politics of recognition, not

8. Hobbes, *De Homine*, trans. C. T. Wood, T. S. K. Scott Craig, and B. Gert, in *Man and Citizen*, ed. B. Gert (Atlantic Highlands, NJ: Humanities Press, 1972), chap. 10, sect. 3–5, pp. 39–43.

from the politics of markets and economic cooperation (understood here as a separate nexus from the politics of recognition, which it wasn't, as Hobbes, like everybody, knew well). Anarchy is the work of vainglory. Hobbes asserts that pride, or *amour-propre*, causes a collapse that requires a union. Since this book is about Rousseau and Smith, not Hobbes, it is worth mentioning that Rousseau repeated this very same argument at the end of the second *Discourse*. One might say that endorsing Hobbes's key argument was one of the purposes of Rousseau's second *Discourse* and was the central part of his criticism of Montesquieu's claim that the combination of *amour-propre* and commerce could be a major stabilizing factor in the underlying social and economic dynamics of modern European monarchies. I will talk about this in later chapters.

In the 1640s, the contemporary challenge to Hobbes was laid on this ground, claiming that the integrative sociability of utility ought to have been kept in the game as an ever-present force that intertwines with the politics of recognition. It will be an important point of my interpretation of Rousseau in later chapters that the politics of recognition was Hobbes's—not Rousseau's or Smith's—invention. The point here is that the idea of commercial sociability had the aim of rescuing the importance of needs, mutual needs, in human society. The idea of commercial society shares on the one hand Hobbes's dismissal of the idea of the *zoon politikon* (and all associated versions of strong sociability that can produce concord) but retreats from Hobbes's statement that the politics of recognition completely overwhelms the integrative forces of utility as an active force of sociability in human associations.

This rescue was first formalized by Samuel Pufendorf. His innovation was to restate this essentially neo-Aristotelian point in Hobbes's own language and, by deploying Hobbes's own method and rhetoric, develop a separate modeling procedure of a state of nature that was geared to explain not the origins of politics and the state directly but the origins of society first. This injection of Aristotelianism into Hobbes's discourse later came to be called socialism because it relied on the foundational presence of society in this firmly utilitarian construction of natural jurisprudence (rather than the thick sociability of the *zoon politikon*). It is not my argument that Rousseau and Smith were socialists. Importantly they were not, and as we shall see, the child of socialism was utilitarianism. In the late eighteenth century it was Cesare Beccaria who was accused of being a socialist by his Christian critics in

Italy. This particular tradition of socialism was renamed as individualism in the early nineteenth century, and in many ways the modern socialists are the heirs not of the original jurisprudential and utilitarian socialists but of their enemies, with the notable exception of Pierre-Joseph Proudhon and Karl Marx, but this is not really the subject of this chapter or indeed this book.[9]

Albert Hirschman suggested that we ought to understand these developments in a sort of Machiavellian or reason-of-state language, such as the contrast between the passions and the interests. The suggestion here is that commercial society had an undergirding conceptual framework based on the contrast and opposition between utility and pride. Strong sociability would be the third term. Instead of the passions versus the interests, one could then talk about the interaction between utility and *amour-propre* as the putative stabilizing factor of modern commercial societies. This is the equation that Kant called "unsocial sociability" and argued that its analysis holds the key to the possibility of developing a social science—that is, a science of society. What Smith described as commercial society is what Kant called unsocial sociability, *ungesellige Geselligkeit*.[10] Kant's term is useful because it makes the concept a deliberate oxymoron, or at least the expression of eclecticism, of a productive compromise. This is the kind of sociability that humanity, made of crooked timber according to Kant's famous metaphor, is actually capable of.

Just like "commercial society," "unsocial sociability" remained a proprietary term, bearing the stamp of an outstanding but idiosyncratic thinker. One does not see it often repeated, if at all. What one sees in the eighteenth century, on the other hand, is the use of proxy terms for these positions. The most important way these proxy terms were used was in building suggestive associations between modern and ancient positions, particularly in moral philosophy. Everybody studied ancient thought

9. On Pufendorf's theory of sociability and eighteenth-century "socialism," see Istvan Hont, "The Language of Sociability and Commerce: Samuel Pufendorf and the Theoretical Foundations of the 'Four-Stages' Theory," in *Jealousy of Trade: International Competition and the Nation-State in Historical Perspective* (Cambridge, MA: Harvard Belknap, 2005), pp. 159–84.

10. Immanuel Kant, "Idea for a Universal History with a Cosmopolitan Aim," trans. A. W. Wood, in *The Cambridge Edition of the Works of Immanuel Kant: Anthropology, History, and Education*, ed. R. B. Louden and G. Zöller (Cambridge: Cambridge University Press, 2007), p. 111.

and the history of antiquity. Modern positions could each be characterized as attempts to revive ancient attitudes. Thinkers could be characterized as neo-Platonic, neo-Aristotelian, neo-Stoic, neo-Epicurean, and
so on. Each could be mixed with or juxtaposed to Christianity. More
importantly, one could see modern controversies as a replay of ancient
ones. Both thesis and antithesis were known, at least in some form, in
advance. Innovations, or the lack of them, could be easily identified.

It is important to call attention to this fact, because it is part and parcel
of recovering the style and thought of the eighteenth century. Methodological caution, however, is in order. In recent scholarship, these neo-
ancient categories have not only been recovered but also been taken as
historically valid indicators of the eighteenth-century positions in moral
and political philosophy they designate. Their historicity cannot be
doubted. The fact is that these adjectives, like Stoic and Epicurean, were
widely used as proxy categories in order to obviate the same difficulty
we are currently encountering—that is, that the naming of positions is
very difficult without attaching them to a historical or pseudo-historical
genealogy. These are and were labeling devices, picking out certain
characteristics of an ancient position and using them to denote a modern
one. Their depth varied, and debates about their precise meaning were
rampant. These labels have to be recovered as proxies, as instruments
of controversy, in the precise depth they were applied. The polemical
use of labels in ancient moral philosophy for modern labeling purposes
is contentious today, and it was disputed at the time. There is no point
treating them with more complexity than they were given when deployed in the eighteenth century. Substituting sophisticated modern re-
constructions of these ancient positions often hinders our understanding
of early modern and eighteenth-century debates, even if they help to
clarify current philosophical meanings and conceptual possibilities. This
technique was of course used by philosophers all the time in the eighteenth century. But to use it beyond this level is not helpful; it is out of
context.

Although Hobbes opened up the discussion of his political philosophy by dismissing Aristotle's idea of a *zoon politikon*, the reconstruction
of the debate about societies without a grounding in sociability eschewed
identification with either Plato or Aristotle. Instead, it was conducted
in terms of a contrast between later Greek or Hellenistic schools of
moral philosophy, usually in terms of a contrast between Epicureans and

Stoics. There were many aspects of Epicureanism and Stoicism that were highlighted, but fundamentally Epicureanism stood for a position in which a foundational sociability of man was missing, or was exceedingly weak, whereas Stoicism stood as a proxy for a theory of sociability. Stoics and Epicureans were moral philosophers, and when the discussion was not about their cosmology, their doctrines were depicted as representing fundamental types of moral philosophy. In this kind of understanding, the Stoics stood for the primacy of virtue and morality over happiness and utility. Epicurus, who was also acknowledged as being a very moral individual, was depicted as making morality instrumental to the achievement of happiness. It was usual for teachers of moral philosophy to start their discussion of morality with this fundamental distinction between ends and means among Stoics and Epicureans. More often than not, the Urtext for this type of discussion was Cicero's *De Finibus* because it contained a comprehensive discussion of both of these positions, including a demonstration of their shortcomings. Adam Smith used *De Finibus* for his History of Moral Philosophy lectures at the University of Glasgow in the 1750s, and so did his near contemporary, Immanuel Kant, when he lectured on the same topic in Königsberg. We shall have an opportunity to look briefly at Smith's use of *De Finibus* later, but as an introduction, it is useful to look at Kant's perspicuous definitions of these ancient schools in his *Lectures on Ethics*.[11]

I am not using Kant here as an authority based on his later critical moral philosophy but as a contemporary controlling text for Smith and Rousseau. Kant, as we shall see later, made space for a proxy for Rousseau in his history of moral philosophy by adding the Cynics and Diogenes in particular to the initial typology of ancient positions. Using *De Finibus* as his point of departure, Kant stated that ancient moral philosophies started off from a definition of the *summum bonum*, or the "supreme good." The supreme good consisted of the physical good and the moral good. Each of these goods was connected by a discussion of means and ends. According to Kant, Epicurus believed that happiness was the end, and morality the means to it, whereas Zeno, the founder of

11. Immanuel Kant, "Moral Philosophy: Collins's Lecture Notes," trans. P. Heath, in *The Cambridge Edition of the Works of Immanuel Kant: Lectures on Ethics*, ed. P. Heath and J. B. Schneewind (Cambridge: Cambridge University Press, 1997), pp. 44–54.

Stoicism, taught the opposite. For the Stoics, morality was the end, and
happiness was a consequence of morality. Stoicism taught the primacy
of morality, whereas Epicureanism depicted morality as a consequence
of pursuing happiness—as something important but secondary. It was
fundamentally this pairing of ends and means in moral philosophy
that provided the underlying matrix of eighteenth-century discussion.
In this debate, the primacy of morality became associated with the primacy of sociability, whereas the lack, or at least the initial lack, of
morality became associated with denying the original sociability of
mankind. As a result, the difference between Stoics and Epicureans was
transformed into an opposition on the issue of sociability as the underlying anthropological category of moral and political philosophy. The
modern canon was constructed accordingly. Hobbes was depicted as
somebody who denied the sociability of man, and hence he was regarded
as an Epicurean. His state of nature was clearly a state in which sociability evaporated or was reduced to an insufficient minimum. Any similar assumption, or even its approximation, was also depicted as Epicurean. Although one doesn't find the expression "commercial society"
often, or many clear analytical discussions of it—perhaps with the signal
exception of Pufendorf—one often encounters accusations of Epicureanism when the merits and use of the concept of the state of nature and
its derivatives were at stake.

This type of direct connection between debates about morality and
debates about sociability was not present in every early modern tradition, but Adam Smith in particular was educated in this very tradition
by his teacher and predecessor at the University of Glasgow, Francis
Hutcheson. Hutcheson, who inherited from his predecessor a natural
jurisprudence and moral philosophy curriculum that was organized, at
least notionally, around Pufendorf's thought, used the concepts of morality and sociability almost interchangeably. He defended both and
described himself as a modern Christian Stoic. He despised and attacked
Epicureanism, which he associated with the position that denied the
primary sociability and morality of man. He clearly nominated Hobbes
as the leading modern Epicurean. Although Pufendorf can legitimately
be seen as a critic of Hobbes and the upholder of Christian sociability,
for Hutcheson he was a Hobbist of sorts, because he adapted Hobbes's
state of nature methodology to the discussion of sociability and therefore, at least in the first instance, derived sociability from utility. Smith
was taught by Hutcheson to dismiss these positions.

Although in academic discourse Hutcheson used Pufendorf as a target, his real enemy was Bernard Mandeville, the Dutch author of *The Fable of the Bees*, whom Hutcheson saw as an enemy of both morality and virtuous politics. Hutcheson saw Mandeville as a dangerous Epicurean. In Ireland, Hutcheson joined a group of republican thinkers and later imported Irish Commonwealth thinking back to Glasgow when he was appointed professor of moral philosophy. In his classroom, the young Adam Smith received a doctrinal introduction into republican politics and Christian neo-Stoic ethics, based on a visceral hatred of commercial society and the kind of thin sociability that was associated with the names of Hobbes, Pufendorf, and Mandeville. Hutcheson described his magnum opus—his *System of Moral Philosophy*, which was the summing up of his teaching career in Ireland and Glasgow—as a farrago, presumably meaning that he took it to be an unsuccessful mixture of philosophical idioms. He probably meant that he could not express his Stoicism and republicanism adequately within the post-Pufendorfian framework that dominated academic natural jurisprudence in his time. But the term helps to separate his moral and political position from the juristic garb in which it was dressed up. His moral and political philosophy and his Christianity cohered well when they were used together to insist on the need for taking a strong and inherently moral position on the importance of generic human sociability.

This is the point at which I want to introduce "Das Jean-Jacques Rousseau Problem," which is the subtitle of this chapter. This is, of course, a joke, but a joke with a serious intent (one that is a bit different from Ernst Cassirer's parallel phrase about the problem—or question—of Jean-Jacques Rousseau). The phrase imitates the so-called Adam Smith problem, which was seen for a long time as the central stumbling block in understanding Adam Smith. The "problem" is the unfortunate consequence of Adam Smith having published two major books, *The Theory of Moral Sentiments* and *The Wealth of Nations*, one in moral philosophy and the other in political economy. The Adam Smith problem is fundamentally about consistency, based on the philosophical assumption that markets and hence theorists of markets lack morality. Based on misunderstandings (and, in fact, on a simple lack of knowledge of *The Theory of Moral Sentiments*), it was supposed to be a genuine discussion of morality and was hence thought to be incompatible with Smith being an enthusiastic political economist of free trade. Consequently, it was supposed that Smith changed his mind between writing the two books, under the influence of the French Epicurean materialists and Physiocrats of the French Enlightenment.

As a biographical story, this scenario was refuted conclusively by the end of the nineteenth century. As a philosophical story, the Adam Smith problem was attributed to obtuse German minds, which is one reason why the phrase (which was coined by the Swiss-based German economist August Oncken in 1898) is now comprehensively out of favor. *The Theory of Moral Sentiments*, it is often pointed out, is an analysis of commercial society, as is *The Wealth of Nations;* the two books analyze the same target. Although this is true, this dismissal of the problem misses the original point. Can we or should we regard commercial society and any analysis of it as moral? How did Adam Smith manage to squeeze in morality on such unpromising foundations? For if he was indeed analyzing a commercial society as the source of morality, he was sailing very close to Hobbist and Epicurean winds. In this case, the two books would be in harmony, as many modern commentators assume, because neither had a moral content. As we shall see, this was the view of *The Theory of Moral Sentiments* held by many of Smith's Scottish contemporaries. Throwing some light on this issue will be the subject matter of some of the comparisons between Smith and Rousseau later in this book.

In some sense, the putative Jean-Jacques Rousseau problem is the opposite of the Adam Smith problem. If Smith was seen as a defender of the commercial realities and politics of his age, Rousseau was widely seen as one of the most uncompromising, if not the most uncompromising, of its critics. If constructing an alignment between moral and political positions about commercial society is correct, Rousseau ought to have been a strong moralist on the anti-Epicurean side. But he was not by any stretch of the imagination that sort of a moralist, an obvious fact that made interpreting Rousseau for most of his friends, then and now, difficult. There was a discrepancy between his moral anthropology and his politics, a sort of inverse of the Adam Smith problem. Interestingly, it was probably Adam Smith who first pointed this out in print. Rousseau's *Discourse on the Origin of Inequality* was published in late April 1755, and Smith's review of this work appeared less than a year later, in March 1756, in the second (and, as it turned out, final) issue of the short-lived first *Edinburgh Review*. Smith was here reviewing the state of French moral philosophy after the achievements of the generation in Britain to which his teacher Hutcheson belonged. Smith claimed that the earlier generation of British moralists was truly innovative, but argued that from the 1740s onward, moral philosophy perked up very interestingly in France, and it was from this quarter that the next wave of innovative work was to be expected. His discussion of Rousseau in this context was longer than that of any other work he reviewed, and unusually for this age, it was frank, analytical, and openly provocative.

Remember that Smith was a dissident pupil of Hutcheson, who had shown that republicanism, a strong position on sociability, and neo-Stoicism added up to a seamlessly unified discourse. Smith saw that the Genevan was a strong republican, who wrote about this political creed with the sublimity of Plato, and he specifically praised the commendable patriotism of the peroration of the second *Discourse*, which Rousseau addressed to his home city. Nonetheless, the high point of the review, its most dramatic statement, was that the underlying moral and theoretical discourse of Rousseau's writing was very similar and possibly indebted to the work of Hutcheson's archenemy, Bernard Mandeville. Smith did not refer to Mandeville as the author of the paradox about "private vices being public benefits." This was the slogan of Mandeville's early work, his attack on Jacobite Fenelonianism in 1704, enlarged upon in 1714.[12] Smith did not assimilate Rousseau to the first version of Mandeville's *Fable of the Bees*. Rather, he pointed to the similarities between the second *Discourse* and Volume II of *The Fable of the Bees*, a separate work from the original *Fable*, which first appeared in 1728 and concluded with Mandeville's 1732 book on the concept of honor and patriotism.[13] While the original *Fable of the Bees* was an attack on Fenelon's *Télémaque*, Volume II was Mandeville's anti-Shaftesbury.[14] It was a work focusing on the foundations of sociability and hence morality. Notably, it was a work that revolved around the notion and vocabulary of *amour-propre*, trying to coin English equivalents to it and innovatively coining iterations of it that could carry the opposite moral meaning. Smith unhesitatingly identified the grounds of Rousseau's position as starting off from a denial of natural human sociability and constructing,

12. On this, see Istvan Hont, "The Early Enlightenment Debate on Commerce and Luxury," in *The Cambridge History of Eighteenth-Century Political Thought*, ed. M. Goldie and R. Wokler (Cambridge: Cambridge University Press, 2005), pp. 377–418.

13. Bernard Mandeville, *An Enquiry into the Origin of Honour; and the Usefulness of Christianity in War* (London: John Brotherton, 1732).

14. See Hont, "Early Enlightenment Debate," pp. 377–418.

like Mandeville, a history that could explain the emergence of the more sophisticated features, moral and cultural, of modern civilization.

He noted that Mandeville and Rousseau came to the topic from a different angle, but the common element was clear: "Both of them suppose," he wrote, "that there is in man no powerful instinct which necessarily determines man to seek society for its own sake."[15] Here was a republicanism that avoided Mandeville's vulgarities but nonetheless started off from the opposite foundations of Hutcheson's republicanism. In terms of the prevailing moral theory stereotypes, this was Epicurean, or Hobbist, republicanism. Smith noted one particular point in the moral foundations where Rousseau criticized Mandeville and improved significantly on the Anglo-Dutch author. Mandeville allowed one other-regarding instinct or feeling in the constitution of man: pity, or the ability to commiserate with the pain of others. For Mandeville, this was a strongly self-centered or selfish behavior. However, Smith noted that according to Rousseau, the underlying mechanisms of pity were capable of producing far more than that, namely virtue—or, more precisely and in the plural, all the virtues or patterns of praiseworthy behavior that Mandeville's selfish system denied. In a mode that comes very close to the sort of position one could associate with Epicureanism, Smith added that for Rousseau, the mechanism that thus produced virtue wasn't a virtue in itself and hence was one that could operate in every human being irrespective of social position. Smith hinted here at a position that produced moral culture without any of the other attributes of one's cultural position in society being high. This, for him, was the foundation of a democratic moral culture in which everybody could participate.

Smith depicted Rousseau as a superior Mandeville and approved of the progress he made over the Dutchman. Arguably, his own work in *The Theory of Moral Sentiments* adopted the same strategy. The cornerstone of the book was an insight by Rousseau, with which he surpassed Mandeville: namely the generalization of the pity mechanism to every conceivable pattern of morality. Any clarification of the Adam Smith problem has to evaluate this attempt—that is, the use of the instinct of

---

15. Adam Smith, "A Letter to the Authors of the *Edinburgh Review*," in *The Glasgow Edition of the Works and Correspondence of Adam Smith: Essays on Philosophical Subjects*, ed. W. P. D. Wightman (Oxford: Oxford University Press, 1980), p. 250.

pity as the archetype of morality as such—as being either a genuine moral theory of a promising kind or a failure because it simply starts from the wrong foundations. The same applies to the Jean-Jacques Rousseau problem. Evaluating Rousseau's republicanism requires clarifying the consequences of this starting point for Rousseau's politics. Rousseau was often depicted in his own time as an Epicurean or a Hobbist, and one ought to investigate the truth in this accusation. In any case, it seems that Smith the political economist and Rousseau, political economy's arch critic, shared moral foundations. This in itself is worth a thorough look.

Smith, however much he praised or appreciated Rousseau's moral departure point, did not endorse Rousseau's political thought. It is not at all clear that he would have deplored Rousseau's republicanism, but he was very critical of the way the two parts of Rousseau's discourse, moral and political, were connected. He described Rousseau's contrasting valorization of the early history of mankind—ending with the opposite conclusion, apparently, to Mandeville's notion of wretchedness—as having been achieved by means of deploying the tools of pastoral novels and painting. This was no praise, just as the rhetorical achievement of sublime Platonism also looks like a sarcastic remark. Rousseau, Smith claimed, did a bit of philosophical chemistry too, which wasn't simply a description, of course, of shrewd textual or conceptual manipulation. Hume used the notion of philosophical chemistry to describe the techniques of the French moralists who developed the selfish system, which demonstrated the hypocrisy of moral life—that is, the selfish motivation behind any and every apparently moral or sociable behavior.[16] In this light, Rousseau appeared as an adept imitator of La Rochefoucauld's or Mandeville's satire, but disguised in the opposite literary genre. Even more importantly, Smith harshly criticized Rousseau's ideas on the origins of justice and politics. He accepted readily the notion that pride or *amour-propre* was a historically developed product. But he dismissed the notion, present both in Mandeville and Rousseau, that justice and government were products of *amour-propre*, the human desire for superiority. The "laws of justice, which maintain the present inequality

16. David Hume, *An Enquiry concerning the Principles of Morals*, in *The Clarendon Edition of the Works of David Hume*, ed. T. L. Beauchamp (Oxford and New York: Oxford University Press, 1998), A2.1–4; SBN 295–97.

amongst mankind," Smith summarized Rousseau, "were originally the inventions of the cunning and the powerful, in order to maintain or to acquire an unnatural and unjust superiority over the rest of their fellow-creatures."[17] Smith did not comment, but anybody who reads his works knows that he disapproved.

The picture is quite clear. If this interpretation is correct, Smith and Rousseau shared theories of moral foundations and possibly some political aims or dreams. There is no real sign of Smith disapproving of republicanism in this review. We also know from a report of the French traveler Barthélemy Faujas de Saint-Fond, who met Smith in 1784, that Smith expressed admiration for Rousseau and apparently told Faujas de Saint-Fond that Rousseau's "Contrat Social will in time avenge him for all the persecutions he suffered."[18] But Smith surely disapproved of the way Rousseau connected the two ends of his project, at least in the text Smith was reviewing, the *Discourse on the Origin of Inequality* (about the peculiarities of this work I shall say more later). Surely, if Smith and Rousseau shared a moral theory, at least up to a point, there were also two different visions of politics attached to the same conceptions of moral foundations and patterns of sociability. More precisely, there were different political theories attached to the moral theory, leading to very different versions of republicanism. Exploring this proposition is the central aim of this book.

⁓ I NOW PROCEED to the very last section of this chapter. One more thing that Rousseau and Smith definitely shared was ambition. They developed very similar plans for grandiose projects in political thought roughly at the same time, in the mid-1750s. Both were deeply impressed and perhaps disturbed by Montesquieu's *Spirit of Laws*. They both felt that it was not sufficiently theorized, or that its theory was submerged beneath a sea of myriad facts and empirical analyses. They both also felt that there was a need for a systematic work on politics that could serve as the equivalent, or better, of Grotius's *On the Law of War and Peace*, the founding text of the modern tradition of natural jurisprudence and international law. When Smith published *The Theory of Moral Sentiments* in 1759, he announced what his next work

17. Smith, "Letter," p. 251.
18. Barthélemy Faujas de Saint-Fond, *A Journey Through England and Scotland to the Hebrides in 1784*, ed. A. Geikie, vol. 2 (Glasgow: Hopkins, 1907), p. 246.

would be. It wasn't *The Wealth of Nations*, although the planned work overlapped with it, and we know that an entire book of *The Wealth of Nations*, Book III, was taken from this project. Smith expressed dissatisfaction with the work of ancient moralists on justice. He also lamented that there was no normative master discourse on which the modern legal systems of nations could depend for development and legal criticism: "It might have been expected that the reasonings of lawyers, upon the different imperfections and improvements of the laws of different countries, should have given occasion to an inquiry into what were the natural rules of justice independent of all positive institution," which could result in a "theory of the general principles which ought to run through and be the foundation of the laws of all nations." And he continued to express his ambition thus:

> Grotius seems to have been the first who attempted to give the world any thing like a system of those principles which ought to run through, and be the foundation of the laws of all nations: and his treatise of the laws of war and peace, with all its imperfections, is perhaps at this day the most complete work that has yet been given upon this subject. I shall in another discourse endeavour to give an account of the general principles of law and government, and of the different revolutions they have undergone in the different ages and periods of society, not only in what concerns justice, but in what concerns police, revenue, and arms, and whatever else is the object of law.[19]

Similarly, Rousseau reported in his autobiography that he intended to write a book on political institutions, in which he wished to answer the great question about the best possible form of government. This required him to answer the question, which he said was not identical with the first but nonetheless followed from it: "What is the Government which by its nature keeps itself closest to the law? From that, what is law?"[20] We know that the second *Discourse*, Rousseau's *Essay on the Origin of languages*, and *The Social Contract* belonged to this project. Rousseau described it as perhaps Grotian in its systematic inspiration

19. Smith, *TMS*, VII.iv.37.

20. Jean-Jacques Rousseau, *The Confessions and Correspondence, Including the letters to Malesherbes*, ed. C. Kelly, R. D. Masters, and P. Stillman, trans. C. Kelly (Hanover, NH: University Press of New England, 1995), book 9, 2.1, p. 340.

but made it clear that he didn't see Grotius and Hobbes as all that different in their concepts of political right. Those who praise Grotius and reject Hobbes, Rousseau wrote, show how little they understand the underlying issues.[21] He did understand, but he never finished the project of overhauling Hobbes.

Clearly the ambitions of Rousseau and Smith were remarkably close, almost identical. Similarly, their work remained unfinished. All that we have, even in proper books like *The Wealth of Nations* and *The Social Contract*, are just fragments. The lost systems probably cannot be reconstructed fully. But their outlines, intentions, and main theoretical thrust most likely can. Such reconstruction ought to happen if we want to understand these thinkers, not just as authors of dead texts but also as presences in our contemporary theorizing. Comparing their politics systematically will probably help. This is the ambition of this book. No doubt my fate in these pages will be the same as that of the two original authors. However, if the point of this project and the need for it become clear, I have already achieved my aim. If one studies the ideological history of our current state form in the West—the ideological origins of the modern representative and commercial republic—one can readily see that it is a result of a synthesis between the work of Rousseau and the work of Smith. If they are compatible at all, it can only be because both were theorists of commercial society. In particular, the political thought of Emmanuel-Joseph Sieyès can be seen as an amalgam of the two, anchored in a theory of commercial society as created by representative labor.[22] If we reconstruct the shape of the lost grand-political-theory projects of Rousseau and Smith, we might be able to pass judgment on this fusion and learn some of the inner secrets of modern statehood as understood after Hobbes.

21. Jean-Jacques Rousseau, *Émile or on Education (Includes Émile and Sophie; or, The Solitaries)*, trans. and ed. C. Kelly and A. Bloom (Hanover, N.H.: University Press of New England, 2010), p. 649.

22. Emmanuel-Joseph Sieyès, "What Is the Third Estate?," in *Political Writings, Including the Debate between Sieyès and Tom Paine in 1791*, ed. Michael Sonenscher (Indianapolis: Hackett, 2003).

~ 2

Commercial Sociability: The Adam Smith Problem

$\mathscr{I}_N$ CHAPTER 1, I argued that Rousseau and Smith shared a common foundation in their moral theory, which justifies us in seeing in Rousseau's moral and political philosophy an analogue to what came to be called the Adam Smith problem. I argued that both accepted as fact the idea that human nature contained no primary or inbuilt principle of sociability that could be the foundation for both morality and politics. Consequently, for both Rousseau and Smith, society had to be supported by other aspects of human nature that could give rise to a secondary kind of sociability, and I suggested that the notion of commercial society was invented to describe this kind of historically produced and in this sense secondary, rather than primary, social formation.

Later in this chapter, I will attempt to describe the kind of politics that can be built on such foundations, on the assumption that both Rousseau's and Smith's politics must be seen as an outgrowth of commercial society. As I noted in Chapter 1, when Smith reviewed Rousseau's most famous and most influential work, the *Discourse on the Origin of Inequality*, he warmly endorsed Rousseau's insight into the foundations of morality but sharply criticized the way Rousseau had attempted to deduce a political theory from it. This critique was not an expression of a value judgment. Rather, Smith objected to Rousseau's failure to develop his history of politics directly from the foundation provided by man's minimal sociability. This critique was the first sign of an important divergence in the way the two men formulated their visions of politics in commercial society. I aim to clarify this issue of political divergence. However, in this chapter, I still want to focus on the close family similarity between Rousseau's and Smith's moral visions. In other words, I am still pursuing the idea that we can draw a worthwhile parallel between the Adam Smith problem and the Jean-Jacques Rousseau problem.

I am starting with Smith and will stay with him for most of the chapter, because in order to be able to conduct a comparative study, I need to format Smith's moral thought in a way that the resemblances to, and the differences from, Rousseau's ideas become easily visible. To my mind, there is a prima facie case for seeing Rousseau's imprint on *The Theory of Moral Sentiments*. Smith's review included three long passages of translation from Rousseau's second *Discourse*, which—without mentioning Rousseau by name—Smith subsequently cited or closely paraphrased in the body of his *The Theory of Moral Sentiments*, specifically in the chapter in which he discusses the role of utility in the formation of a developed commercial economy.[1] I will return to the content of these direct instances of controversy with Rousseau in the parts of this book that deal with the connections between politics and economics. Here I would like to indicate a much more obvious place in *The Theory of Moral Sentiments* that shows a direct imprint of Rousseau, namely the very beginning. In his review, Smith highlights the greatest advance that Rousseau had made over Mandeville, who Smith sees as Rousseau's predecessor, as follows:

> Mr. Rousseau however criticises upon Dr. Mandeville: he observes, that *pity*, the only amiable principle which the English author allows to be natural to man, is capable of producing all those virtues, whose reality Dr. Mandeville denies. Mr. Rousseau at the same time seems to think, that this principle is in itself no virtue, but that it is possessed by savages and by the most profligate of the vulgar, in a greater degree of perfection than by those of the most polished and cultivated manners.[2]

1. Smith, *TMS*, IV.I.10.
2. Adam Smith, "Letter," p. 251.

The opening passages of *The Theory of Moral Sentiments* repeat this very idea loudly and clearly. In the very first sentence of the book, Smith presents the reader with the idea that pity is an entirely natural other-regarding mechanism built into human nature:

> How selfish soever man may be supposed, there are evidently some principles in his nature, which interest him in the fortune of others, and render their happiness necessary to him, though he derives nothing from it except the pleasure of seeing it. Of this kind is pity or compassion, the emotion which we feel for the misery of others, when we either see it, or are made to conceive it in a very lively manner.[3]

He then repeats the idea that he had already underlined in the review essay, namely that pity is not a civilizational achievement or an effect of civilization but that it is present in all human beings, not just in the sentimentally refined ones:

> That we often derive sorrow from the sorrow of others, is a matter of fact too obvious to require any instances to prove it; for this sentiment, like all the other original passions of human nature, is by no means confined to the virtuous and humane, though they perhaps may feel it with the most exquisite sensibility. The greatest ruffian, the most hardened violator of the laws of society, is not altogether without it.[4]

Next, Smith explains that pity is a spectatorial phenomenon that is not confined to instances of actually observing sorrow and pain, insisting that its logic could be generalized. According to Smith, compassion is not confined to observations of deadly calamities but could embrace all human emotional reactions in every kind of situation:

> Neither is it those circumstances only, which create pain or sorrow, that call forth our fellow-feeling. Whatever is the passion which arises from any object in the person principally concerned, an

3. Smith, *TMS*, I.i.I.1.
4. Ibid.

analogous emotion springs up, at the thought of his situation, in the breast of every attentive spectator.[5]

Finally, Smith suggests that the generic name for the general phenomenon he describes should be sympathy, rather than pity or compassion, even if this usage was somewhat counter-intuitive for most ordinary language users:

> Pity and compassion are words appropriated to signify our fellow-feeling with the sorrow of others. Sympathy, though its meaning was, perhaps, originally the same, may now, however, without much impropriety, be made use of to denote our fellow-feeling with any passion whatever.[6]

I argue that we need to format Smith in a way that the similarities to Rousseau's ideas become clear. The prelude to *The Theory of Moral Sentiments* loudly advertised the idea that Smith had singled out as the most enthralling of Rousseau's ideas in his review of the second *Discourse*. Anybody who knew Smith's review, at least in Scotland and among his friends, could readily recognize this fact.

Before I proceed to reconstruct the core argument of *The Theory of Moral Sentiments*, I would like to underline the historical basis of my interpretation even further. Many on the continent, particularly in Switzerland, recognized in Rousseau's denial of human sociability a kind of Epicureanism, and they also noted his lack of warmth toward the cause of the social virtues. The nineteenth-century German commentators on Smith, who called attention to real or imagined inconsistencies between his moral philosophy and his economics, were the inheritors of a similar idea, namely that political economy was an inherently Epicurean—that is, a fundamentally unmoral—discourse. I want to show that this was also the view of the majority of Smith's Scottish contemporaries. For them, there was no "Adam Smith problem" of inconsistency. *The Theory of Moral Sentiments*, they realized, was instead cut from the same "selfish" cloth as *The Wealth of Nations*. By simply running through some of the contemporary reactions to *The Theory of Moral*

5. Ibid., I.i.I.4.
6. Ibid., I.i.I.5.

Sentiments, we see that Smith's contemporaries refused to accept Smith as a serious moral theorist. Here is what Adam Ferguson wrote:

> You endeavour to explain away the distinction of Right and Wrong by telling us that all the difference is the Sympathy or want of Sympathy, that is, the Assent and Dissent of some two or more persons of whom some one acts & some other observes the action and agrees or does not agree in the same feeling with the actor.[7]

Did Smith really mean, Ferguson asked, that the distinction between right and wrong did not exist when such reactions did not take place and were not observed? "Does the presence of any sympathy ascertain a good action, or the want, of a bad one?" he further asked.[8]

Smith's successor in the Chair of Moral Philosophy at Glasgow, Thomas Reid, was even more outspoken. He denounced his predecessor as follows:

> It is evident that the ultimate Measure & Standard of Right and Wrong in human Conduct according to this System of Sympathy, is not any fixed Judgment grounded upon Truth or upon the dictates of a well informed Conscience but the variable opinions and passions of Men. So that we may apply to this System, what Cicero says of the Epicurean. "So your school undoubtedly preaches the simulation of justice instead of the real and genuine thing."[9]

According to Smith, he continued, "Social Virtue seems to be resolved either into Vanity or into self-interest."[10] Although in the Smithian view "all Our moral Sentiments are resolved into Sympathy," Reid stated, "so even this Sympathy seems to be resolved into self love, which receives some change in its direction by an operation of the imagination."[11] Thus,

---

7. Adam Ferguson, "Of the Principle of Moral Estimation," in *On Moral Sentiments: Contemporary Responses to Adam Smith*, ed. J. Reeder (Bristol: Thoemmes Press, 1997), pp. 92–93.

8. Ibid., p. 93.

9. Thomas Reid, "A Sketch of Dr. Smith's Theory of Morals," in Reeder, *On Moral Sentiments*, pp. 81–82.

10. Ibid., p. 77.

11. Ibid., p. 70.

"Dr Smith's System of Sympathy," he concluded, summing up his criticism, was "wrong. It is indeed only a Refinement of the selfish System."[12]

Dugald Stewart, who was chosen as the memorial lecturer by the Royal Society in Edinburgh after Smith's death, was plainly embarrassed by *The Theory of Moral Sentiments*. He summarized it as best he could, or as far as it was possible, but he deeply disagreed with the book's argument. Imagine how strongly he must have felt about this if he was compelled to state this in the midst of an official eulogy.[13] In his university lectures, Stewart repeated Reid's charges against Smith: Smith's theory, he told his students, "may account for a man's assuming the appearance of virtue." This was not an unimportant subject, he added, for it was "the real foundation of the rules of good breeding in polished society."[14] This particular disparaging phrase he borrowed from James Beattie, the professor of moral philosophy in Aberdeen. The meaning was clear. Smith had written a theory of politeness, not of morality; perhaps a moral sociology, but not a true moral philosophy. Smith, Stewart further charged, used the word "sympathy" inconsistently and vaguely and had

mistaken a very subordinate principle in our moral constitution (or rather a principle superadded to our moral constitution as an auxiliary to the sense of duty) for that faculty which distinguishes right from wrong.[15]

"It may be objected to Mr. Smith's theory," he argued damningly,

that it confounds the means or expedients by which nature enables us to correct our moral judgments, with the principles in our constitution to which our moral judgments owe their origin. These means or expedients he has indeed described with singular penetration and sagacity, and by doing so, has thrown new and most

12. Thomas Reid, "Letter from Thomas Reid to Lord Kames," in Reeder, *On Moral Sentiments*, p. 66.

13. Dugald Stewart, "Account of the Life and Writings of Adam Smith LL.D.," in *The Collected Works of Dugald Stewart*, ed. W. Hamilton, vol. 10.

14. Dugald Stewart, *The Philosophy of the Active and Moral Powers of Man* (Boston: Wells and Lilly, 1828), p. 228.

15. Ibid., pp. 225–26.

important lights on practical morality; but, after all his reasonings on the subject, the metaphysical problem concerning the primary sources of our moral ideas and emotions, will be found involved in the same obscurity as before.[16]

Stewart picked up Smith's assertion that man was not inherently sociable or moral and that these features of moral behavior were not present in early or solitary humans. The implication was that in Smith's view, without society, morality could not develop. This might be true, Stewart admitted, but it was not sufficient to invalidate the presence of an inbuilt human moral capacity that remained dormant in those circumstances.

It has recently become fashionable to say that *The Theory of Moral Sentiments* was a very important and famous book in its time. This is true, but it must not be taken to be an index of approval, acceptance, or even understanding by Smith's contemporaries. *The Theory of Moral Sentiments* was difficult and was often denounced, then as now, as a dead end for the further development of moral philosophy.

More importantly, it was regarded as an Epicurean work. Of course, the prevalence of this view does not mean that it was fully or even substantially correct. Dugald Stewart himself mentioned in his lectures that for years Smith had lectured successfully on Cicero's *De Finibus*, and these lectures became the backbone of the late additions to *The Theory of Moral Sentiments*, which are now known as Smith's history of moral philosophy. No lecturer on *De Finibus*, however, could be simply an Epicurean or, of course, a Stoic. The whole point of *De Finibus* was the dialectical play between the two systems, showcasing the inadequacies of both. Smith might have had more leanings toward Epicureanism than some others, but he could not be simply an Epicurean. What Smith's critics meant by Epicureanism was probably what Kant explained in his classification of eighteenth-century moral teachings, also using *De Finibus* as his guide. From this perspective, what annoyed his critics was that for Smith, virtue was not the telos of man, as it was for the Stoics, but the means, the instrument of a happy and good life, as it was for the Epicureans.

We should not be surprised by the sharp contemporary criticisms of Smith. Although the arguments of these Scottish critics were certainly

16. Ibid., pp. 227.

hostile, they were not groundless. Smith himself admitted to, or rather proudly asserted, the very same things. He described the modern moral philosophy debate as having been started by Hobbes and then developed through the controversy between Hobbes and the Platonists (Ralph Cudworth, the Cambridge Platonist, was the first who answered Hobbes). There is no reason to think that Smith would have positioned himself as a Platonist or, even for that matter, as a Stoic. Rather, he portrayed himself as someone who had properly developed the Hobbesian stream—that is, the selfish system (Hobbes, La Rochefoucauld, Pufendorf, Mandeville, and Hume were the named members of this tradition)—to its proper conclusion, shedding the vulgar and mistaken elements adopted by the early representatives of this doctrine. Smith made no secret of the fact that sympathy, as he understood it, was the truly central moral category of the amended selfish system. He wrote as follows:

> That whole account of human nature, however, which deduces all sentiments and affections from self-love, which has made so much noise in the world, but which, so far as I know, has never yet been fully and distinctly explained, seems to me to have arisen from some confused misapprehension of the system of sympathy.[17]

It was this initial misinterpretation of sympathy that *The Theory of Moral Sentiments* was intended to correct. Hence, by self-definition, it was a treatise in enhanced Hobbism and Epicureanism. For the party of virtue, this road led to a cul-de-sac. For them, the selfish system could never be improved enough to pass moral muster. For those who were on the other side, Smith's book was of major interest. What makes Smith interesting is that he was probably the most fascinating thinker, together with Rousseau, who worked on rescuing moral discourse from the selfish system without abandoning its basic insights. What was his intellectual strategy to achieve this ambitious aim? Smith's system was fascinating, but it was also relatively complicated. As Dugald Stewart already complained bitterly in his memorial lectures, *The Theory of Moral Sentiments* was difficult to summarize.

Smith knew his history of moral philosophy. He was absolutely right in claiming that sympathy had been an essential element in arguments

---

17. Smith, *TMS*, VII.iii.I.4.

concerning sociability and human nature for at least a hundred years before he wrote. It was present in Hobbes, and Pufendorf indeed referred to Hobbes when he introduced it into his own concept of sociability. If, Pufendorf claimed, "in seeking out the true Condition of Men we have assign'd the first Place and Influence to Self-Love," this was not out of approval of a morality founded on selfishness but in recognition of the simple fact that every man was naturally "sooner sensible of the Love he bears towards himself, than of that which he bears towards others."[18] Self-regarding and other-regarding motives were not in rigid opposition; they could be combined. Pufendorf dubbed this insight as a Stoic argument, but he cited it from Hobbes's *De Cive*: "When a Man doubts whether what he is going to do to another be agreeable to the Law of Nature, let him suppose himself in the other's room."[19] This technique of role switching, of projecting one's intended actions on the situation and feeling of others, if repeated and multiplied, resulted in sociability. The system of sympathy was grounded on a process of envisaging one's predicament in a network of mirrored reciprocities. What Smith set out to do in *The Theory of Moral Sentiments* was to generalize it, soften it, embellish it, and strip it of all foreseeable tendency to corruption.

Sympathy was based on "complacency," not in the modern sense of the word but in the old meaning of occupying the same place (*cum-placere*) with others through compassion, feeling together with others. These notions were discussed with unusual intensity in the academic and philosophical culture from which Smith came. That is why Smith could recognize the close similarity between Rousseau's *Discourse on the Origins of Inequality* and Volume II of Mandeville's *Fable of the Bees* with such a sure touch. He had already rehearsed all these arguments in the controversies that surrounded the work of Hutcheson, his teacher. He could spot precisely what Rousseau had done with pity because he was already traveling down the same road himself. The nature of sympathy and complacency, their precise position in the selfish system, was a subject of protracted and heated controversy between Hutcheson and Mandeville and then between Hutcheson and some of his contemporary critics, such as John Clarke and Archibald Campbell, who forced

18. Samuel Pufendorf, *The Law of Nature and Nations*, ed. J. Barbeyrac, trans. B. Kennet, 5th ed. (London: J. and J. Bonwick, 1749), 3.2.14.

19. Ibid., 7.1.14.

Hutcheson to modify his position on self-love and sympathy from edition to edition of his moral treatises on the passions and virtue.[20] Hutcheson's opponents often sound as if it were Smith who was talking. In any case, they were clearly discussing the same kinds of points Smith would address in *The Theory of Moral Sentiments*. The same applies to David Hume, who was a sophisticated sympathy theorist in his own right. When one talks about Rousseau's impact on Smith, one is not talking about a radical and broad break in Smith's development. Rousseau probably helped Smith more easily decide that the way ahead was through the generalization of the pity model, but otherwise his system was probably already in place in 1755. The minds of Smith and Rousseau could meet because they were both intervening in the most central moral theory debate of their time.

Smith clearly stated in *The Theory of Moral Sentiments* that his aim was to correct Hume. His explicit reference was to Hume's doctrine of justice. Hume assumed that utility could generate moral behavior if it was channeled through the agency of taste and guided by the desire of mental order. Utility pleased aesthetically, stripping selfish sentiments of their directly utilitarian and selfish undertones. Smith accepted the main drift of Hume's idea but objected to the complicated mechanism of understanding that was implied by the activity of discovering the beauty of complicated utilitarian instruments, as in seeing the beauty of a society whose institutions were geared to stabilizing justice. This could not be the archetype of justice, Smith claimed, because its complicated modus operandi made it an aristocratic and rarefied activity.[21]

Smith drove back the discourse to locate the origins of justice in basic passions, such as resentment (which is why he is sometimes interpreted as having abandoned the traditional focus on social justice in favor of focusing on criminal justice, an inexplicable howler on the part of some modern interpreters). This interest led him into the territory of Hume's most famous (and, for many contemporaries, his most Epicurean) theory,

20. Hutcheson's first major work was the 1725 *An Inquiry into the Original of Our Ideas of Beauty and Virtue*. Hutcheson's ideas were criticized in John Clarke's 1726 *Foundation of Morality in Theory and Practice Considered* and Archibald Campbell's 1728 (and reissued with many alterations in 1733) *An Enquiry into the Original of Moral Virtue*. In 1728, Hutcheson published *An Essay on the Nature and Conduct of the Passions and Affections*, which considered the criticisms of Clarke and Campbell, modifying his view in some dimensions, as well as making revisions to the *Inquiry* in its subsequent editions through to 1738.

21. Smith, *TMS*, IV.1.1–2.12.

namely the idea that justice is an artificial virtue.[22] Humans, Hume claimed, have no inbuilt sense of justice, since one can easily think of a number of limiting cases when justice, as normally understood, was not kept and would have made little sense if chosen as a guide. Justice was a natural but also a historically developed phenomenon, and Hume provided his readers with a beautiful conjectural or theoretical history of the birth of justice and its gradual experimental development by way of the hit-and-miss discovery of progressive paths of advancing it, until the utility of these avenues to justice became apparent to everybody. Justice was not a product of a contract but had been created through the emergence of initially uncoordinated social collaboration by trial and error. These discoveries were guided by narrow instrumentality, as on a boat in which the rowers develop a unison movement of pulling their oars in the same direction and at the same pace in order to make efficiency gains, based on no more explicit agreement than the tacit understanding of the manifest utility that could be derived from their joint effort of disciplined rowing, also facilitated by the historically evolved purposeful design of both the boat and the oars. Smith, it seems, was impressed by this idea, and he decided to apply it to the explanation of the development of sympathy.

The Theory of Moral Sentiments is best read as a natural or theoretical history of sympathy in the Humean mold. Smith applied the explanatory mechanisms offered by Hume's theory of the origin of justice to the rise of moral rules in society in general. He not only generalized pity but also historicized it. This move paralleled Rousseau's *Discourse on the Origin of Inequality* in many ways. Smith's natural history of sympathy was a parallel to Rousseau's history of self-love, his conjectural history of *amour-propre*. *The Theory of Moral Sentiments* was Smith's conjectural history of the origins of commercial society through sketching out the mechanisms underlying the rise of the sociable self.

Both Smith and Rousseau had to construct histories, because without natural sociability, all sociability had to be artificial—that is, developmental (or "adventitious," in the older technical language of natural jurisprudence). For Smith, humans were originally no more than

---

22. David Hume, *A Treatise of Human Nature*, in *The Clarendon Edition of the Works of David Hume*, ed. D. F. Norton and M. J. Norton (Oxford: Oxford University Press, 2007), T.3.2.1–6; SBN 477–534.

physical beings, with dormant or exceedingly undeveloped psychological capacities. Solitary humans could not develop their psyche
while remaining solitary. Nor could such creatures be aware of their
own humanity. They could see themselves in the mirror of a puddle
but could not judge their own appearance: were they beautiful or ugly,
harmonious or deformed? Were they like others, or were they different?
These things could be discovered only through comparison, by meeting
others in fellowship. Smith, like everybody else, took it for granted that a
human had both a body and a psyche, or soul, with needs and capacities
in both dimensions. The psychological capacities were mostly elementary building blocks of sentiments or passions, such as anger.
Smith also assumed, taking a leaf from Hobbes and going back to the
faculty psychology of Aristotle's rhetoric, that humans had a primitive
judging faculty, not of judging good and evil as Hutcheson and others
had insisted on but of judging each other, more particularly of judging
each other's deformities or other divergences from the norm. This
presupposed a desire for superiority or, as Smith keenly emphasized,
a desire for avoiding being judged as inferior.

For humans, the opinion and criticism of others mattered. This was
constitutional to human nature: a put-down caused psychological pain,
and just as all animals wished to avoid pain, humans wished to escape
from each other's primitive critical judgment. No doubt Smith knew
Hutcheson's bitter criticism of Hobbes's theory of laughter, and he put
it to good use in his own theory.[23] By meeting others, humans discovered their own physical and mental inadequacies and became aware of
their aversion to being censured. This judging principle of humans was
clearly aesthetic; it was incipient taste. In response, humans developed
a desire to please others. This was a prudential response to the pervasive presence of humans constantly comparing themselves with one another. The rise of the comparative human self, or briefly the human self,
and its psychological needs then overwhelmed the initial physical needs
of the physical or solitary self. The same point was also made emphatically by both Hobbes and Rousseau. Next, Smith described how the
human quest for internal psychological balance and external recogni-

23. Francis Hutcheson published three short essays on laughter in the *Dublin Journal* in
1725, the first of which was a refutation of Hobbes. These are collected in Francis
Hutcheson, *Reflections upon Laughter and Remarks upon The Fable of the Bees* (Glasgow: R. Urie,
1750).

tion became the seedbed of inequality. Respectability conveyed superiority. It was these psychological needs and pathologies that explained the rise of social stratification, or the origin of ranks.

Man's judgmental nature was a central plank of Smith's theory of the self, responsible for a range of psychological outcomes. To escape judgment by their fellows, individuals had to adapt to others. This led to socialization, the formation of shame, and hypocrisy. This was the first line of psychological defense and what the critics of the selfish system saw as the origin of fake virtue. These developments, however, did not diminish individual competitiveness; they only channeled it into new modes of behavior. The real remedy would have been to diminish dependence on *amour-propre* by leaving the game of intensely competitive comparative judgment altogether. The most important protective shield for psychologically vulnerable individuals (meaning, in fact, everybody) was self-approbation or self-esteem, the reversal of the other-directedness of the self. This was the only road not to false but to genuine virtue. As Smith pointed out, moralists were inclined to invent many avenues of psychological defense against competitive psychological anarchy, such as feelings of humanity, benevolence, love of mankind, and love of neighbors. These were all feeble agents. Anxiety in the face of the opinion of others had to be controlled, Smith argued, by the love of self, the love of our own virtue.

This was the road that led to the argument of trusting the judgment not of others but of an impartial spectator and of using his or her judgment as a weapon of self-defense. This required the acquisition of a source of judgment that imported a balanced and normalized appraisal by society as a whole into the inner realm of the psychological armory of individuals. The impartial spectator was a device for the inner regulation of one's own self—in other words, a facilitator of self-command. It is often claimed that self-command was a Stoic virtue; it was not so for Smith. His was no heroic virtue based on a tough theory of the government of the soul. If anything, it was an Epicurean theory of self-command. It consisted of a reduction of primitive selfishness and self-aggrandizement by reducing our own selfishness to a level acceptable to other selfish agents. As Smith wrote:

It is not the love of our neighbour, it is not the love of mankind, which upon many occasions prompts us to the practice of . . .

virtues. It is a stronger love, a more powerful affection, which
generally takes place upon such occasions; the love of what is hon-
ourable and noble, of the grandeur, and dignity, and superiority of
our own characters.[24]

In this model of mitigated or sophisticated self-love, being sure of
one's own superiority—or, at any rate, of one's impregnable position in
the face of others—was paramount. It required the achievement of normalized psychological self-sufficiency, which depended on knowing the
content of social norms. Smith phrased this requirement as follows:

> We suppose ourselves the spectators of our own behaviour and en-
> deavour to imagine what effect it would, in this light, produce upon
> us. This is the only looking-glass by which we can, in some mea-
> sure, with the eyes of other people, scrutinize the propriety of our
> own conduct.[25]

This allowed Smith to reformulate the concept of self-command in
terms of a competitive adjustment of the positive golden rule. In effect,
he inverted the rule, adapting it to the requirements of the selfish system:

> To feel much for others and little for ourselves, that to restrain our
> selfish, and to indulge our benevolent affections, constitutes the
> perfection of human nature; and can alone produce among man-
> kind that harmony of sentiments and passions in which consists
> their whole grace and propriety. As to love our neighbour as we love
> ourselves is the great law of Christianity, so it is the great precept
> of nature to love ourselves only as we love our neighbour, or what
> comes to the same thing, as our neighbour is capable of loving us.[26]

Note the foundations of Smith's strategy. The issue for him is always
the balance, or propriety, one can establish between self-regarding and
other-regarding sentiments. It is a fully sentimentalist theory in the
technical sense of the term. But unlike many other sentimentalists of

---

24. Smith, *TMS*, III.3.4.
25. Ibid., III.1.5.
26. Ibid., I.i.5.5.

his period, Smith never preoccupies himself with how love is to be increased in society. Instead, he wants primitive self-love to be decreased. Self-love, *amour-propre*, should be decreased, muted, self-controlled (Smith is wholly against outside control), but not replaced. Practically everything comes from self-love. But self-love was as complex as society itself. Remember the definition of commercial society as a society that was less coherent, less glutinous and trouble-free, than a society based on love and intentionally purposeful cooperation. What Smith worked out was a definition of commercial society in terms of moral psychology.

The aim of all individuals was to obtain independence from the criticism of others in conditions in which the love they offered to others and the love that others offered to them was less than apparent. Individuals had to live within themselves but at the same time live in society. They had to import the norms of society into their own bosoms as a tool of survival rather than abandon themselves to a vain search for approval by others. The idea was attractive, but only if this kind of self-judgment could be made reliable. Smith often pointed to the terrible dangers of self-deceit, self-justification, or an enhanced selfishness adopted as a shield of protection irrespective of the facts of the situation and the opinion of others.

Here too he deployed the same strategy of argument. His solution was to work out the possibility of a yet higher level of self-command, one that could overcome the forces of self-deception. The formation of one's defense against external judgments of one's self had to be stabilized by accepting rules of self-judgment that were grounded in social norms. A rule adopted this way was a device that could help detect self-deception, mitigating the atavistic urge to opt for defensiveness at all cost. It is at this point that the parallels between *The Theory of Moral Sentiments* and Hume's theory of artificial justice become clear. Individuals could avoid self-deception only with the help of rules based on norms. These general rules of morality could only be formed by—and be based on—the long and sustained historical experience of individuals judging others and being judged by others in society. These rules, imported into our psyche, created the impartial spectator within our breast. This impartial spectator within ourselves was, therefore, our savior from the psychological warfare of all against all that characterized human societies.

Knowing the rules, meaning the social norms, could correct self-deceit. Knowing only the rules, however, was not sufficient. To make such rules a tool of self-control, mental recognition needed reinforcement. Smith deployed a whole battery of arguments in this direction, and here I cannot go further than just listing them. Religion for Smith was a social institution that was invented to shore up moral norms. Further up in the developmental sequence it was moral theory, or moral science, that helped our moral self-defenses operate decently and under control. On the whole, Smith was not in favor of the passions controlling passions. Nor was he in favor of their suppression. He put his trust as a theorist in the working of the human imagination through sympathy, tracking its development from its primal physical foundations—as can be seen in his theory of generalized pity. Sentiments were always at work, pleasing and displeasing individuals constantly, as the psychological vibes of society ebbed and flowed, contracted and spread. Here Smith emphasized the role of psychological pain, which was the real punishment for breaking moral rules and the sanction for the departure from social norms. On top of the torment of the primary punishment, secondary reinforcement came from Humean quarters—from happiness and utility or, in general, from the regulative effect of having or not having success in society. Taking a leaf from Shaftesbury, Smith also emphasized the therapeutic nature of polite sociability and conversation in society for reducing anxiety, which in turn could help humans live with one another.

We shall have an opportunity to discuss the wider consequences of these Smithian ideas. The emphasis on psychological need in Smith was strong, perhaps as strong as in Hobbes, although the details had changed considerably. Politically, Smith was helped by his emphasis on psychological democracy. Glory seeking created inequality among individuals. This, however, was not only an affliction of successful elites. Every human being was subject to it and lived under its sway, including the working class. Their response to the forces of pride—or esteem seeking—and their constant desire for betterment had as great, if not greater, an impact on popular politics as it did on those who enjoyed the privileges of the system.

I have presented Smith in a way that makes the similarity between his concerns and Rousseau's highly visible. Now I want to turn to Rousseau and present him in a way that makes the similarities between the preoccupations of the Scot and the Genevan equally clear. One avenue would be to point out that both came from Calvinist societies, where the major theological–philosophical debate of their time revolved around attempts to tone down the doctrine of original sin and enlighten, literally (for "Enlightenment" is a theological term), the history of fallen mankind. This was the drift of Hutcheson's attack on the selfish system, and Rousseau came from the equivalent Swiss background. Another avenue would be to point out biographical parallels. Rousseau's and Smith's lives overlapped, but in strictly generational terms, Rousseau was a contemporary of Hume, not Smith. Smith was one generation younger, which explains a great deal about their work in a comparative perspective. Smith's starting point was Hume's skepticism toward the theories of Hutcheson, and it was this that helped him identify Rousseau's ideas in the *Discourse on the Origin of Inequality* as traveling along parallel trajectories to those of Hume. One can also approach the Rousseau–Smith encounter through Smith's interest in rhetoric and modern literature. Smith recognized that Rousseau was a supreme stylist and rhetorician, but he also saw his gift as a poisoned chalice.

In a few cases, Rousseau's formulations were very effective, but it was easy to mishear them, despite his explicit and frantic efforts to counter immediate misreadings of his work (it is an extraordinary assumption to believe that only later generations misunderstand, whereas contemporaries do not). One particularly salient example is Rousseau's apparent statement that man was naturally good, and that it is only commercial society (society built on *amour-propre*, comparative self-love) that causes evil and corruption. Consequently, it is widely—but wrongly—believed that for Rousseau, socially constructed self-love was a purely negative agency in human history. But for Rousseau, as for Smith, this was the absurd mistake that some of their predecessors' efforts to overturn the doctrine of fallen human nature had drifted into. Recently, vigorous attempts have been made to recover from this misunderstanding by pointing out that for Rousseau, *amour-propre* was the glue of society, good and bad, and that it stood at the origin of culture and morality as much as of corruption and excess. This is perfectly obvious if one considers both Rousseau and Smith as theorists of commercial society, a form of society that lacks primary human sociability but builds everything (both good and bad, by definition) out of the needs of selfish individuals having to live together. Those who have then tried to recover Rousseau's attempts to save the selfish system have pointed out that the mirroring and role-switching mechanisms that Rousseau began to describe could have allowed him to explain how the feelings and judgments involved in *amour-propre* could become a working moral enterprise of sorts. The claim in this chapter is, in fact, that Rousseau started to develop this system. And, whether or not it is right to describe this as Rousseau's possible project, it was indisputably Smith's actual project. This in fact is literally the case: Smith takes these ideas from the second *Discourse*, discovers their relevance for destroying Hutcheson's and Shaftesbury's heritage (they are not identical, and the same volume of the *Edinburgh Review* that included Smith's review of Rousseau included a comparative study of Hutcheson and Shaftesbury, contrasting their starting point as a benevolent system for Hutcheson and a selfish system for Shaftesbury, exploding the misunderstanding that their thought was closely aligned or identical), sees what Hume does to the discourse, and sets out to write a whole book about it. Roughly speaking, the book that Rousseau should or could have written, according to these modern interpreters of Rousseau's *amour-propre*, is, mutatis mutandis, *The Theory of Moral Sentiments*. Rousseau pointed out the way, but importantly he didn't do it. Smith did. Hence, we are given two visions of politics in commercial society, but to this I will come later.

Yet another and perhaps more promising avenue for comparing Rousseau and Smith would be to point out the morphological similarities between *The Theory of Moral Sentiments* and the second *Discourse*. Once we recognize the core of *The Theory of Moral Sentiments* as a natural history of sympathy, the similarity to Rousseau's natural history of *amour-propre* will appear obvious. Hume's version, also showcased in his *Natural History of Religion*, did not establish a European paradigm, but Rousseau's second *Discourse* definitely did. It created the new genre of the histories of mankind. (Usually Isaak Iselin, who was Swiss like Rousseau—although not from Geneva but from Basel, another commercial republic—is credited with inventing the genre with his *History of Mankind*. His work was arguably a direct answer to Rousseau, expressing, as it were, the Swiss equivalent of the Hutcheson side of the Scottish argument.) Reinhart Koselleck, following a hint from Carl Schmitt, denounced this kind of history as the nemesis of real history and perhaps the most poisonous legacy of the Enlightenment.[27] This

27. Reinhart Koselleck, *Critique and Crisis: Enlightenment and the Pathogenesis of Modern Society (1954)* (Cambridge, MA: MIT Press, 1988).

judgment is correct in the sense that Rousseau's and Smith's theoretical histories were not actual accounts of recorded history but moral and political philosophy presented in a historicized form. But for philosophers, this "historical" genre was also problematic. It was this very historicity, as against direct normativity, that was described as Epicurean. In this idiom, morality was conceived of as instrumental and hence fragile. It could not survive without being shored up by politics, and it is this reliance of moral theory on politics that I will follow up in later chapters. My immediate interest at this juncture is to discover why it is that the directly parallel or identical trajectories of Rousseau's and Smith's theoretical histories of the social self have remained practically invisible to their readers for such a long time. I want to show how the second *Discourse* was directly catapulted, wrapped in the historical or quasi-historical idiom in which it was constructed, into the very epicenter of the defense and critique of the selfish system that I identified as Smith's proximate target. This will bring me to Montesquieu, another distinguished player in the very same moral-theory debate to which Hutcheson, Hume, Rousseau and Smith, and many others all over Europe were contributing (with the Neapolitan Vico being yet another outstanding, but earlier, author in the very same genre).

What follows is a quick trot, perhaps even a gallop, over the capacious terrain of Montesquieu's thought, for which I put up signposts instead of explicating arguments in detail. Rousseau, in his two famous *Discourses*, answered questions set by the academy of Dijon. He answered them broadly, but he was also always on target. The first question, on whether the Renaissance had improved Europe's morals or not (the Renaissance was then called the revival of the arts and sciences), elicited a gargantuan response of conjectural history. The second question, on inequality, was practically a direct question about the moral status of modern monarchies. It is often believed that Montesquieu had a tripartite theory of regime classification. This is wrong. In fact, he had a double system of dualities. He first divided regimes into rightful and despotic ones, into regimes of laws and regimes of personal power. In the second duality, he divided lawful regimes, *rei publicae*, into two kinds, one based on equality (republics or collectively ruled regimes) and the other based on inequality.[28] A *res publica* based on social inequality is

---

28. Montesquieu, *The Spirit of the Laws*, ed. A. M. Cohler, B. C. Miller, and H. S. Stone (Cambridge: Cambridge University Press, 1989), pt. 1, bk. 3.

what Montesquieu called a monarchy, a vertically stratified republic. This was perfectly obvious to anybody who ventured to write about politics in the second half of the eighteenth century. Asking a question about inequality was asking a question about monarchies (in contrast to democratic or aristocratic republics). Montesquieu's great innovation was to argue that egalitarian and inegalitarian *rei publicae* not only had different forms of government but also rested on different moral cultures. Famously, he claimed that egalitarian republics had to be based on a moral culture of the suppression of the self.[29] This statement makes sense only if one assumes human nature to be selfish. Equality required individuals to exercise self-command in order to correct their own selfish tendency (this was the subject of Rousseau's book *The Social Contract*, which explains how control of the selfish self had to be selfish itself, but collectively so). In monarchies, inequality was a systemic feature, and self-command aiming at equality was not necessary (Montesquieu scandalized his readers by suggesting that, politically speaking, it was even harmful). Instead, the selfishness in commercial society had to be reined in by pitting varieties of selfishness against one another. Montesquieu's best definition of the moral culture of a modern monarchy was a metaphor of the planetary system, in which gravity was not able to pull the planets into the sun.[30] The gravity was selfishness, namely the selfishness of utility-guided market behavior. It could be neutralized by *amour-propre*, pride, the psychological need for recognition. When codified and institutionalized, pride or grandeur seeking became a system of honor, or, as Montesquieu emphasized, of false honor, false glory, a mere love of superiority without moral worth.[31] This notion was derived from Montesquieu's considerable knowledge of the Jansenist tradition in France, which was an Augustinian Christian version of the same theory, and was possibly enhanced by reading the articles published on the system of passions in Joseph Addison's contemporary English magazine, the *Spectator* (although the key essay was authored not by Addison but by the Welsh minister Henry Grove).[32]

29. Ibid., pt. 1, bk. 3, chaps. 2–5.
30. Ibid., pt. 1, bk. 3, chap. 7.
31. Ibid.
32. Hont has in mind Henry Grove's September 1, 1714, article (No. 588) in the *Spectator*; see Istvan Hont, "The Early Enlightenment Debate on Commerce and Luxury," in *The Cambridge History of Eighteenth Century Political Thought*, ed. M. Golide and R. Wokler (Cambridge: Cambridge University Press, 2005), p. 405.

Montesquieu's theory of monarchy in *The Spirit of Laws* was the terminal stage of the "Tale of the Troglodytes," which he had begun over twenty years earlier in his *Persian Letters*. The tale began with the Troglodytes' establishment of a regime of pure love and then a regime of pure selfishness.[33] It posited the voluntary transformation of the Troglodyte system of love into a luxurious monarchy once the inhabitants got tired of suppressing their true—that is, selfish—selves, with their incipient *amour-propre*. The theory of modern monarchy, as Montesquieu presented it, stated that stable regimes must rest on the balance of love and selfishness, honor and utility, and this arrangement required the cultivation of an honor system. It was Rousseau's avowed aim in the second *Discourse* to blow Montesquieu's theory of modern monarchy out of the water by demonstrating that such a society could not escape a Hobbesian outcome and that once the society was constructed commercially, not even the Hobbesian devices could stabilize it. He predicted a pendulum of Caesarism and democracy in Europe through a devastating sequence of never-ending revolutions, following a pattern of cyclical crises. Montesquieu defined modern monarchy as a moral culture of mitigated selfishness, of self-checking *amour-propre*, at least under some institutional circumstances. The second part of the second *Discourse* provided a history of *amour-propre* to disprove this thesis as a pious and ill-grounded hope.

Commercial society, Rousseau argued, could not be stabilized through the psychodynamics of hypocrisy that was the pervasive culture of monarchy. The masterpiece of the politics of the eighteenth century that Montesquieu described could not work. Smith subsequently provided an alternative theoretical history of *amour-propre*, reviving the hope that it might work if it were allowed to operate properly. *The Theory of Moral Sentiments*, from this perspective, was the beginning of Smith's own answer to both Montesquieu and Rousseau.

My very last point in this chapter addresses the issue in Part I of the second *Discourse*. The second part of the second *Discourse* begins with a pure theory of commercial society in which there is no or little sociability but a great utilitarian need for cooperation. This was the standard overture to all theories of commercial society. Rousseau's was not essentially different, although he made a whole range of fascinating

33. Hont discusses Montesquieu's tale of the troglodytes in "The Early Enlightenment Debate on Commerce and Luxury," pp. 405–7.

modifications. The standard idiom displayed commercial society as the human predicament as such, or, if the author was Christian, the predicament of fallen mankind. The favored device was to show commercial society's necessity through a comparison between man and animal. Animals were instinct driven and had a strong but narrowly directed self-love, *amour de soi-meme*, which guaranteed their survival if circumstances allowed it. Humans, in contrast to animals, were not physically equipped for practical survival. The compensating element was their ability to learn and to change themselves because they had brains and psyches, which made them capable of generating artificial sociability. Society was the great human advantage over animals, and social mankind was indeed capable of surpassing animals on such a large scale that the initial comparison between them, which showed animals in a favorable light, would become meaningless. But the price to pay for this selfish economic dynamic was inequality.

Rousseau was determined to pull the plug on the first premise of this theory, namely that inequality rested on hard-wired features of human nature. Rather, he claimed, inequality was a product of history, more precisely the history of the social self, or of *amour-propre*. In the beginning, humans were not disadvantaged vis-à-vis animals; they were just as strong as them. The thesis of human weakness or imbecility was a mistake or an ideology. Humans had extra potential over animals from the beginning, but it was dormant. Without society, without sociability, humans were practically animals. They were vicious when trying to survive, but also good because they had no other aims. They had no moral intentions, because morality had to be generated through social interaction. As a good student of Montesquieu, Rousseau gave a geographical dimension to this idea and identified the origin of humanity in the tropical climes of Africa, where survival for prehuman humans was easy. Commercial society was a feature not of southern but of northern societies, where the human-weakness thesis was manifestly true. Rousseau posited that the dispersion of mankind from the South to the North was a result of natural catastrophe, an ecological disaster that had cut the original link between the creatures and their natural habitat. In their new habitat, they needed society to survive, just as had been claimed by other political thinkers.

The precise psychogenesis of this sort of society was not described in the second *Discourse*. Rousseau only hinted at the problem, because the psychogenesis of society also required explaining the birth of the communicative vehicle of society, namely language. He described it in the second *Discourse* as a chicken-and-egg problem that he could not solve (this spurred his readers to figure it out for themselves—Smith was one and Herder, famously, was another who responded). Hence, the natural history of society and *amour-propre* remained very sketchy and truncated in the second *Discourse*, making the similarities with Smith more difficult to spot. It is at this point that I want to remind you of what I have said about the virtually identical avowed ambition of both Smith and Rousseau, namely reconceiving Grotius's and Hobbes's politics in terms of a post-Montesquieuan comprehensive theory of law, society, and politics. To capture its outlines in Smith, one needs to see *The Theory of Moral Sentiments* as a natural history of sympathy. Concomitantly, Rousseau's parallel effort becomes clear if one considers what I call his "third discourse," on the origin of languages, which was almost certainly a part of the original text of the second *Discourse*. This text was a history of the move from Africa to the North and the formation of society via language in between. Language arose from symbolic egoism and through playacting and music. It had an aesthetic epistemology, not a utilitarian one. This aspect was not captured by the history of northern utility-based commercial societies, but its shape was much more similar to Smith's purely conjectural history of the sympathetic self, without geographical shifts and other considerations intervening in the description. To a degree, Smith moved along a similar trajectory to Rousseau's *Essay on the Origin of Languages*, which can now be seen as the missing link between the first and second part of Rousseau's *Discourse on the Origin of Inequality*. As Dugald Stewart emphasized, perhaps the most lasting contribution of Smith to moral theory was to block the road to utilitarianism and socialism (in the old jurisprudential sense). Smith was an intentionalist in moral theory, but he grounded it in a refined version of the selfish system. Politics was a complicated consequence of selfish human nature. Not until we see its psychological foundations fully (and I will talk about these, even if only briefly, in later chapters) can we even think of seriously comparing Rousseau's and Smith's politics.

～ 3

Histories of Government: Which Comes First, Judges or the Law?

I WILL NOW PROCEED to explore some agreements and disagreements between Rousseau and Smith. The agreement is in their common denial of the natural sociability and morality of man. To focus on the disagreements, I want to start by returning to that paragraph in Smith's review of Rousseau's second *Discourse* in which an explicit disagreement was registered. The paragraph in question states that both Mandeville and Rousseau "suppose the same slow progress and gradual development of all the talents, habits, and arts which fit men to live together in society, and they both describe this progress pretty much in the same manner."[1]

Smith agreed, for he later adopted a similar approach to these phenomena. In the review, however, the next step gave rise to criticism:

According to both [Mandeville and Rousseau], those laws of justice, which maintain the present inequality amongst mankind, were originally the inventions of the cunning and the powerful, in order to maintain or to acquire an unnatural and unjust superiority over the rest of their fellow-creatures.[2]

1. Smith, "Letter," p. 250.
2. Ibid., p. 251.

48

Smith did not embellish this comment because the point he was making was initially about the surprising similarity between Mandeville's and Rousseau's texts. But he did disagree. In fact, he staked his entire later oeuvre on his disagreement with this account of the origins of justice. Instead of following this style of argument, Smith's natural history of sympathy was modeled on Hume's natural history of justice. One might indeed argue that the radical departure was actually Hume's. Smith followed him in this path, but not slavishly. The title of this chapter—"Which Comes First, Judges or the Law?—was designed to capture the nature of his achievement. For Smith, the issue was not simply to restate the fact that justice and government were artificial, because Mandeville and Rousseau also claimed this, but to construct a natural history of both justice and government. Hume wrote a natural history of justice, and Smith attempted a natural history of government. To repeat, the issue was not simply the artificiality of politics but the nature of its artificiality. To capture this, one needed to understand the nature of its genesis and history.

On this issue, there was a stark contrast between some of Smith's and some of Rousseau's fundamental statements. Let's take the *Discourse on the Origin of Inequality* first. Having described the origins of property and the social contract, Rousseau argued that "nascent Government had no constant and regular form":

> Society consisted of but a few general conventions which all individuals pledged to observe, and of which the Community made itself guarantor toward each one of them. Experience had to show how weak such a constitution was, and how easily offenders could escape conviction or punishment for wrongs of which the public alone was to be both witness and judge; the law had to be eluded in a thousand ways, inconveniences and disorders had to keep multiplying, before it finally occurred to them to entrust the dangerous custody of the public authority to private individuals, and to commit to Magistrates the task of getting the People's deliberations heeded.[3]

3. Jean-Jacques Rousseau, "Second Discourse," in *The Discourses and Other Early Political Writings*, ed. V. Gourevitch (Cambridge: Cambridge University Press, 1997), p. 175.

This all sounds familiar. There were man-made, not natural, laws at the earliest stage of society, and when the law was not observed, then and only then was there a further need to create a legal authority in society to enforce the law. Rousseau was adamant that this was the right way of sequencing the history of the human creation of justice: first there was the law and only afterwards the emergence of judges or magistrates. "For," he wrote in the second *Discourse*, "to say that the Chiefs were chosen before the confederation was established, and that the Ministers of the Laws existed before the Laws themselves, is an assumption not worthy of serious refutation."[4]

Smith took a diametrically opposite view. In his *Lectures on Jurisprudence*, and also in Book V of *The Wealth of Nations*, which was based on his Glasgow jurisprudence lectures, he discussed the huge opposition to the introduction of Roman courts in conquered German provinces:

> The courts of justice when established appear to a rude people to have an authority altogether insufferable; and at the time when property is considerably advanced judges can not be wanted. The judge is necessary and yet is of all things the most terrible. What shall be done in this case?[5]

Although it might at first seem that Smith took a line very similar to Rousseau's, he in fact advanced the opposite theory. These societies created the first judges out of necessity. But the power of judges was resented and feared, and a remedy had to be found for this fear. Judges needed to be brought under control and their activities regularized by codifying the rules that the judges claimed they were interpreting. "This was the case at Athens, Sparta, and other places," Smith wrote, "where the people demanded laws to regulate the conduct of the judge, for when it is known in what manner he is to proceed the terror will be in a great measure removed." He drew the lesson from this in direct opposition to Rousseau. "Laws," he declared,

> are in this manner posterior to the establishment of judges. At the first establishment of judges there are no laws; every one trusts to

4. Ibid., p. 176.

5. Adam Smith, *Lectures on Jurisprudence*, in *The Glasgow Edition of the Works and Correspondence of Adam Smith:*, ed. R. L. Meek, D. D. Raphael, and P. G. Stein (Oxford: Oxford University Press, 1978), p. 314.

the natural feeling of justice he has in his own breast and expects to find in others. Were laws to be established in the beginnings of society prior to the judges, they would then be a restraint upon liberty, but when established after them they extent and secure it, as they do not ascertain or restrain the actions of private persons so much as the power and conduct of the judge over the people.[6]

The disagreement with Rousseau in this case is incontrovertible, and I assume that here Smith was in fact consciously arguing against Rousseau. The issue, as Smith clearly stated in this passage, was the interpretation of liberty. Although they might not have had sharply diverging views on liberty, it seems that they definitely disagreed on the issue of how liberty and hence political society were created. Their histories of modern liberty and law diverged, and this eventually led to divergent political views. Since they shared the same starting point—the lack of natural sociability—their divergent histories of the origin of law led to divergent visions of politics in commercial society. Where did this divergence originate from, and what did it amount to?

On the very same page that Rousseau announced his views about the proper sequencing of the origin of judges and the law, he explained that the people decided to appoint judges and chieftains to enhance their own liberty, and not in order to enter into slavery or dependence. This was Smith's point too. Nonetheless, they saw two crucial issues differently. The first issue was their understanding of the nature of conventions and their histories. In other words, they differed in their ideas concerning the concept of a social contract. Hume famously undermined this idea as a picture of historical reality, although he acknowledged its compelling normative logic.[7] Smith faithfully reproduced Hume's critique of contractualism in his Glasgow lectures.[8] His purpose, and Hume's, was not to reject the idea of a social contract but to replace the contractual history of legal and political normativity with a more plausible historical account. (We should note that "history" here refers to

6. Ibid., p. 314.
7. Hume, *Treatise of Human Nature*, T.3.2.7–10; SBN 534–67; Hume, "Of the Original Contract," in *Essays Moral, Political and Literary*, ed. E. F. Miller (Indianapolis: Liberty Fund, 1987).
8. Smith, *Lectures on Jurisprudence*, pp. 315–17, 402. Hont discusses Smith's deployment of Hume's arguments against Lockean contract theory in "Adam Smith's History of Law and Government as Political Theory," in *Political Judgement: Essays for John Dunn*, ed. R. Bourke and R. Geuss (Cambridge: Cambridge University Press, 2009), pp. 138–40.

theoretical history—that is, conceptual sequencing along a timeline—and hence the importance of the debate between Rousseau and Smith about the proper sequencing of the emergence of judges and the law.)

Hume's idea was to replace the contract with a compact—a tacit agreement expressed through actual cooperative practices that had emerged over time through trial and error. It was precisely this type of thought that undergirded the idea that judges exist before the law. One able individual solved a dispute between individuals. When he was asked to do this again and again, he de facto became a judge. Once the utility of this practice became visible to the majority, a system and a principle had been created. When the practice of judging by experts became widespread, the practice had to be normalized and its principles codified. Hume emphasized that this kind of normalization of distributive procedures was not justice for all situations, but it was a necessity for needy individuals who lived in conditions of moderate scarcity and were of roughly comparable physical and mental capabilities.[9] For them, the need for survival dictated the invention of private property, and in the very same process they created the institution of justice. For Hume, justice and property were coterminous categories.

It was at this juncture that Rousseau and Smith diverged. When Rousseau explained the creation of chiefs and judges, he pointed out that the people chose superiors for themselves in order to gain something from this exchange rather than accept that they were losers. In the case of property, Rousseau could not see what sort of advantage was present for the people. For property divisions to survive for a longer period, voluntary acceptance was needed. Private property could not be stabilized if it were simply an injustice foisted on the people by superior force. This meant that Rousseau had to try another route. But voluntary acceptance of such an unfavorable condition for the majority was possible only if the people were duped by seductive rhetoric. Private property as a legalized system was born of a confidence trick, and this fact was bound to influence the growth of society negatively forever. Inequality of private property had a tendency, Rousseau claimed, to grow and disrupt any political arrangements based on it. Rousseau painted a bleak future of oscillation between despotism and egalitarianism, creating a reiterated cycle, or gyration (as the eighteenth century termed it), of political instability. This was not Smith's view.

9. Hume, *Enquiry concerning the Principles of Morals*, 3.1–7; SBN 183–86.

Smith disagreed not because he was starry-eyed about private property and inequality. In fact, he was a stern critic of both. He accepted, however, that the system of commercial society had a long-term beneficial tendency, creating more and more equality and material well-being for the majority. This was clearly not Rousseau's view in the *Discourse on the Origin of Inequality*. Why did they diverge?

Both Rousseau and Smith created a natural history of justice and society to explain the origins of law and politics. In fact, they both accepted the same parameters for their theories as did Hume. They were interested in justice for needy humans under conditions of moderate scarcity, meaning, in other words, under the political and economic conditions of Western Europe, including perhaps some of the Mediterranean area, such as Greece. They were therefore interested in the genesis and history of societies that inhabited temperate climates. Theoretically speaking, in terms of Rousseau's second *Discourse*, they were interested in the history of societies in which the cause of human association was physical need.

Both Rousseau and Smith began their modeling of the history of morality and government by taking Hobbes's anti-Aristotelian denial of primary human sociability as their starting points. Like Hobbes, they saw that humans had both physical and mental needs and that the mental ones were hugely powerful and disruptive. This was why the satisfaction of mental needs—recognition seeking—was a central issue for human societies. Hobbes focused on the containment of mental needs, essentially pride or glory seeking, through politics. Arguably Rousseau and Smith saw the interaction between material and mental needs as more proximate, ongoing and developing, and because of this, they kept the economic or utility-based structure of society more at the forefront of their social thought than did Hobbes. Whereas Hobbes excluded sociability and utility from the foundations of politics, those who followed him wanted to bring back some of these factors for various purposes, only some of which are of interest to us here. One interesting mode of argument was that of the French Augustinians, the so-called Jansenists. They started from a strong version of the Christian doctrine of fallen man and accepted Hobbes's solution of political artifice in the earthly city as a mitigation of the disorders generated by the Fall. Their idea of fallen man was very similar to Hobbes's asocial or antisocial man. Fallen man was a creature without love or charity, wholly preoccupied with glory seeking and concupiscence, but still living in society. From this angle, commercial utility appeared to work as a mitigating secondary socializing factor that could help to stabilize the political system and put a lid on the endless rivalry fueled by mental neediness.[10] Montesquieu's idea of modern monarchy belonged to this family of political argument. A Jansenist critic of French absolutism, such as Pierre Nicole, saw clearly that the disciplinary sovereignty of the sword was not sufficient for establishing lasting order. Discontent and competition had to be neutralized by more than the naked exercise of power; instead, it had to involve mainly catching fallen men on the hook of utility—or, more precisely, accepting glory seeking and concupiscence as mingled with and expressed through utility. Respect for wealth and the desire for material splendor as an outward sign of individual glory, both thoroughly corrupt sentiments, had irresistible power over the minds of fallen men. Under the disciplinary tutelage of the state as the guardian of justice, utility and pride could be combined in such a way that the outcome would be directly conducive to the peace and improvement of society. The essence of this kind of argument was to retain the characteristic Hobbesian point about the dominance of the politics of recognition over the purely material, physical, or economic nexus of society. Thus, in the case of the Jansenists, Hobbes's idiom was intertwined with Christian theology. Both Rousseau and Smith, on the other hand, stepped back to the more pure and original Hobbesian (or Epicurean) idiom, and many of their contemporaries saw this very clearly. Indeed, it is only fairly recently (I mean in the twentieth century) that political theorists have lost the ability to identify these idioms with any clarity.

Rousseau wanted to demonstrate that the Jansenist-Montesquieuan solution did not improve on Hobbes but instead destroyed the force of his doctrine of sovereignty. As he went on to argue, the combination of commercial utility and recognition seeking was bound to push Hobbes's state into excesses of centralization while still rendering his kind of politics unstable (it is in this Rousseauian mirror that it becomes quite clear that Hobbes was not, and could not have been, a theorist of politics of the modern commercial kind). Smith, like Hume, took the opposite tack, insisting that absolute government was unnecessary if the dynamics between the politics of recognition and utility seeking were allowed to

10. Hont discusses the French Jansenists in "Jealousy of Trade: An Introduction," in *Jealousy of Trade*, pp. 46–51.

play themselves out fully within a framework of justice and legality. As Hume insisted, politics had two underlying principles: liberty and authority. Hobbes, he claimed, was a great innovator in the theory of political authority, but because of the peculiar political situation of his time, he overemphasized authority. Good political theory had to keep both liberty and authority jointly in play.[11] Rousseau and Smith made the same case about the relationship of authority to liberty. Some commentators have argued that Rousseau took anti-Hobbism too far by swinging politics away from authority and toward liberty. This view, however, has virtually no merit. To understand the overriding relevance of law to politics, Rousseau claimed, one had to understand the relationship between liberty and authority in the development of human society very precisely. Smith made the same claim in his history and theory of law and government. Both set out to build a historicized theory of this grand theme—that is, the possibility of lawful authority—in very similar terms.

Utility in this discourse was given several meanings. One was liberty, particularly in Hume's and Smith's usage. It also stood for society created through need, as an economic nexus. Politics that had a grounding in utility, not just in authority, relied on a concept of society conceived as a mode of economic interaction. For a long time, Smith's readers saw this as the only visible element of his underlying political system. Those who looked for the antecedents of Marx discovered his four stages theory, which classified governments and other social institutions according to the mode of living or the mode of subsistence that defined the underlying society. Smith famously listed four such stages: the hunting–gathering stage, the shepherd or pastoral stage, the stage of agriculture, and the stage of commerce. We know that he had developed this style of theorizing even before he published his *Theory of Moral Sentiments.* When Smith returned from Oxford to Scotland, his first mode of subsistence was to give evening classes in Edinburgh under the patronage of Henry Home, Lord Kames—a landowner, literatus, and senior Scottish judge. We know little about the lectures, but Smith gave two series, one on rhetoric and belles lettres, a kind of aesthetics course, and one on the history and principles of jurisprudence. His four-stages theory first appeared in the latter and chimed both with the interests of the Scottish elite after the 1745 Jacobite scare and with Kames's ideas

11. Hume, "Of the Origin of Government," in Miller, *Essays Moral,* p. 40.

in particular, since he was attempting to modernize Scottish law and clean it of its feudal remnants. It was in order to argue that as society changed, the law too had to change, that this kind of jurisprudential theory first surfaced in this intellectual environment. It is customary to identify the intellectual origins of this kind of stages theory in the modern natural jurisprudence tradition, particularly in its theories of property rights and in ideas concerning economic improvement, stretching back to ancient Roman thinking about agriculture and estate management. The discourse also bore the mark of the tremendous influence of Montesquieu's *Spirit of Laws*, which was a treatise arguing for legal and administrative reform, authorizing legal change if it was in harmony with the spirit of the underlying society. Smith's friends consistently argued that he had in fact taken up not the challenge of Grotius but that of Montesquieu when he set out to write his historical theory of law and government. This was Smith's plan for his second book after *The Theory of Moral Sentiments* (it was not *The Wealth of Nations* but an unpublished book that Smith had burned after he died). He announced this in 1759, in *The Theory of Moral Sentiments*.[12] One might think that for chronological reasons one must see the law and politics project as an extension and continuation of Smith's moral philosophy, as is often the case in modern American thought. But it is possible to conceive of the sequence of the intellectual genesis the other way around. *The Theory of Moral Sentiments* was the kind of moral theory it was (we saw that many contemporaries dismissed it as social, not moral, theory) because it was already a prologue to the law and politics enterprise that Smith had embarked on. The only evidence we have of Smith's thinking in 1755—the year he wrote his review of Rousseau—is a fragment that is now lost but was still available to Dugald Stewart when he wrote his memorial lectures of Smith in the early 1790s. The fragment dealt with political reform and free trade in a key reminiscent of French theorizing in the first half of the eighteenth century. What I am suggesting is that the natural history of sympathy in *The Theory of Moral Sentiments* had the same structure as Smith's natural history of the law. Both centered on people judging one another and building defenses against harsh judgment—the one in individual terms, or morally; the other in institutional terms, or legally. In both cases, Smith used Hume's natural his-

12. Smith, *TMS*, VII.iv.37.

tory of justice as an artificial virtue as his archetype. Unlike Rousseau, Smith refused to make use of the idea of contract as a constitutive element in forming his account of the birth of legality as a switch from fact to right, from history to normativity, from "is" to "ought." (Hume was not actually against getting from "is" to "ought," although he criticized improper ways of thinking about it.)[13] In his anti-contractarianism, Smith followed Hume, whereas Rousseau still followed Hobbes. We will never know what would have happened if Rousseau had also read Hume. To clarify the Rousseau–Smith comparison even further, one would need to understand the Hume–Hobbes relationship properly (Hume attacked Locke, not Hobbes), but this is not my subject. Here, one might use the Hegelian term *Aufhebung* (literally "lifting up") to describe it because there is a dialectic of debate at work in the interaction. Hutcheson attacked Hobbes, and Hume attacked Hutcheson; hence, Hume willy-nilly restated some of Hobbes's ideas at a higher or more properly digested and philosophized level. Smith, who rebelled against Hutcheson, his original teacher at Glasgow, also followed this kind of dialectic. For both, improving on Hobbes had to entail the elimination of the contractual element from the natural history of the state.

Let's return to the idea that the reemphasizing of utility in politics, reemphasized after Hobbes's attack on it, resulted in a stages theory of history structured according to economic organization. Smith is famously associated with this move. Rousseau's moves in the same direction have, however, attracted much less attention. But let us listen to Rousseau in the third discourse, the one on the origin of languages, particularly those parts that were originally written for the second *Discourse*, the *Discourse on the Origin of Inequality*. "Human industry," Rousseau argued in this text, "expands with the needs that give rise to it":

Of the three ways of life available to man, hunting, herding, and agriculture, the first develops strength, skill, speed of body, courage and cunning of soul, it hardens man and makes him ferocious. The land of the hunters does not long remain that of the hunt. Game has be pursued over great distances, hence horsemanship. Game that flees has to be caught, hence light arms, the sling, the arrow, the javelin. The pastoral art, father of repose and of the indolent

13. Hume, *Treatise of Human Nature*, 3.1.2.27; SBN 469–70.

passions, is the most self-sufficient art. It almost effortlessly provides man with food and clothing; It even provides him with his dwelling; the tents of the first shepherds were made of animal skins: so were the roofs of the ark and the tabernacle of Moses. As for agriculture, it arises later and involves all the arts; it introduces property, government, laws, and gradually wretchedness and crimes, inseparable for our species from the knowledge of good and evil.[14]

This is not that different from Smith's stages theory. The similarities become even clearer when Rousseau draws his conclusion from this description of the three stages of economic development:

> The preceding division corresponds to the three states of man considered in relation to society. The savage is a hunter, the barbarian a herdsman, civil man a tiller of the soil.
>
> So that regardless of whether one inquires into the origin of the arts or studies the earliest morals [or ways of life, *moeurs*] everything is seen to be related in its principle to the means by which men provide for their subsistence, and as for those among these means that unite men, they are a function of the climate and of the nature of the soil. Hence the diversity of languages and their opposite characteristics must also be explained by the same causes.[15]

The sections of the discourse on languages in which these ideas appeared were meant to fill the gap in the story of mankind depicted in Parts I and II of the second *Discourse*. In this context, Rousseau rephrased his famous complaint about the ahistoricity of Hobbes's model of the state of nature. He described it as the European fallacy to assume that the history of mankind took place in Europe alone. Quite the contrary, he argued, mankind came from tropical, hospitable climates, thus from Africa. There, the standard assumptions of initial human weakness or imbecility did not apply. European history was a consequence of a displacement, a break in the link between the human animal and its natural habitat, due to a disaster or some other natural event that led to

---

14. Rousseau, "Essay on the Origin of Languages," in Gourevitch, *Discourses and Other Early Political Writings*, pp. 271–72.
     15. Ibid., p. 272.

physical migration from one climate to another. Thus, the standard story certainly did apply to Europe, but not to the entirety of mankind. European society was indeed created by need and utility. "Help me!" was the plaintive cry of one human to another, Rousseau claimed, when asking for society and the assistance of his or her fellows. But what happened to the people of the original South? Had they no society because they had no fatal weaknesses and hence no real need for one another? Had their human potentials and passions been bound to remain dormant forever? Was no artificial sociability developed in Africa? Was there no human need for recognition? This was the part of the story that Rousseau famously left unresolved in the text of the second *Discourse* because of the dilemma built into establishing the origin of language as the primary vehicle of sociability. In the essay on the origin of languages, he had a go at this problem.

The first stage of the narrative remained a story of utility. Society could only be created where humans regularly met. Even in Africa, this had to be due to some physical need. This was still a basic animal need, as Rousseau emphasized, for animals in Africa behaved similarly. He identified the necessity in question as the need for water, caused by thirst. Africans met at rivers, at oases, and wells. Once they met, however, they started to diverge from animals, for they compared themselves to one another and recognized their humanity, as belonging to the same species. They started to develop a primitive comparative social self. In the second *Discourse*, Rousseau demonstrated the sudden rise of *amour-propre* at the village Maypole feast, an icon of communitarianism in European culture, and demonstrated that the incipient lookism of humans created a competition leading to winners and losers, and hence resentment and revenge. The same story in the essay on languages applied to Africans who met at the watering hole on the savanna. They created society not out of the need to satisfy their physical needs in cooperation, for the water was a natural and common source, and drinking was an individual activity, but out of the psychological need for recognition, out of *amour-propre*. Their plaintive cry was not "Help me!" but "Love me!"

Speech started as a gesture for recognition, a song and a melody. The sociability of speech was the child not of economic but of cultural need, structured by an underlying aesthetics of the human mind, by a quest for love and order, fueled by a wonderment of nature and other humans.

Smith shared these ideas fully. But this is not the point that is of immediate interest here. According to Rousseau, speech was of a southern and tropical origin, and its development preceded the enforced human migration to the North. Those who reached the North and found their human physicality sorely wanting in the new environment could already speak and hence ask for help. For Rousseau, human language in the North was ruined by the demands of harsh living in an inappropriate environment. What happened there was that the society of recognition was overlain by the society of mutual need, of utility. The consequences were tremendous, both good and bad. For better or worse, northern history was patterned by need and hence by the mode of economic living. In the South there were no stages of history, just one stage. History as a developmental process was a northern invention.

Both Rousseau and Smith were primarily interested in telling this northern and European story, which was the story of development. Neediness required an effort to overcome it. This effort led to intellectual development, the unlocking of dormant human capabilities. It also led to changes in the use of the human environment. Necessity was the mother of invention. In the North, both material and psychological needs drove men forward. It was the intertwining of the two—of the society of love and the society of need—that provided the source of the dynamics (please note the term "love" in both *amour de soi-même* and *amour-propre*—these were loves, not reasons or ideas). Before one could think about living happily, one first had to think about living in the sense of surviving. In Rousseau's own words:

> Mutual need united men far more effectively than sentiment would have done, society was formed solely through industry, the ever-present danger of perishing did not permit of a language restricted to gesture, and their first word was not *love me* but *help me*.[16]

Smith claimed that Rousseau (and before him Mandeville) could not fit the origin of laws into this developmental story. Rousseau understood that justice was artificial, not natural. In other words, if it was conventional, then it had to be invented by convention. The logical archetype, or ideal type, of a convention was a contract. Hume, and following him

16. Ibid., p. 279.

Smith, begged to differ. While Hume sketched out the outlines of an alternative idea, Smith set out to write its natural history. He claimed that a proper legal regime, which he termed a republic, or *res publica* (in the capacious sense that allowed both republics in the narrow sense and monarchies to be *rei publicae*, which is the same way that Montesquieu and Rousseau used the word, as too did Hobbes), first emerged in classical antiquity—in Greece and then in Rome. He claimed that this development was the result of a long and complicated history. It did not start with the invention of the law as such, which then became the subject of a long process of ever more elaborate institutionalization. Quite to the contrary, there was a long gradual institutionalization process that culminated in the idea of the law (or right) as such. The underlying structuring mechanism of the emergence of law was the intensification of society. It was accepted that society itself was held together by need. As we have seen, Rousseau modeled his stages theory similarly. He wrote:

> Everything is seen to be related in its principle to the means by which men provide for their subsistence, and as for those among these means that unite men, they are a function of the climate and of the nature of the soil.[17]

Further, Rousseau linked the rise of legality to the third stage: "As for agriculture," he wrote,

> it arises later and involves all the arts; it introduces property, government, laws, and gradually wretchedness and crimes, inseparable for our species from the knowledge of good and evil. Hence the Greeks viewed Triptolemus not merely as the inventor of a useful art, but as a founder and a wise man to whom they owed their first education and their first laws.[18]

Smith shared this view completely, but he went one step further. Rousseau did not talk about a fourth stage, but he knew what it was: the rise of urbanization, the city, with its dense population and ever-increasing

17. Ibid., p. 272.
18. Ibid.

frequency of exchange processes. Smith identified the rise of legality, the *Rechtsstaat* if you prefer, with Greece—not only with the rise of Greek agriculture, although it started there, but with the founding of the city, the polis, in Athens. He identified ancient Athens as a fledgling urban or commercial society.

I have still not discussed in detail how Smith demonstrated that there were first judges and that only after this came the law. This encompassed the first two stages of social development, hunting–gathering and shepherding. The reason for this is that I am keen to show how similar were the roots of Rousseau's and Smith's thoughts. They were both elaborating ideas of Montesquieu. The author of *The Spirit of Laws* also started his explanation of Greek developments by pointing to geographical factors. Rousseau was fascinated by this. The cradle of politics in Greece was in Attica, which was not the most but in fact the least fertile part of the country. There was a need for a combined effort there, and the results were magnificent. Smith described the rise of Greek legality and Greek agriculture as a premature or special instance of the transition from the shepherd to the agricultural stage and then to the urban-commercial mode of living. This was not part of a global or even a continent-wide sociopolitical transformation but an avant-garde development that created an island of progress in the sea of shepherd life that was to continue uninterrupted in Asia and most of Europe. This is why the legality of the ancient republics was eventually destroyed by the shepherd nations that surrounded them (one can already see here that the story is not purely economic but also very importantly military).

A truly epochal and systemic transition from shepherd to agricultural (and later commercial) politics occurred only in modern European history. In Greece, the transition from shepherding to agriculture was an important but isolated phenomenon, determined by geographical accident. The early Greeks, an Asiatic-type shepherd nation, conquered the relatively infertile landmass of Attica, which had clear natural borders, allowing for an easy defense of the territory. The lack of space forced the Greeks to replace shepherd life with the sedentary practice of agriculture, which led to rapid economic development. The Greeks developed a surplus, and this in turn favored artisanal industry and commerce. This economic progress had momentous consequences. Their wealth, Smith argued, required a strong defense. Thus, Greek politics first changed not under the sway of an economic logic but as a result of the security problem this wealth gave rise to. Attica was protected from Asia by mountains but had an unprotected sea frontier. Against pirates, the best defensive response was to collect the whole population into a well-protected walled settlement. In this way, the Greeks invented the agricultural city-state or republic, and urbanization changed Greek politics dramatically.

Previously, the Greeks had a post-shepherd community structure. Each village had its own chieftain. In the city, however, none of the former tribal chieftains could dominate the others; no citywide chieftain could emerge and establish a shepherd monarchy. Further, since space was limited, the crowded nature of the city made the vast inequality that characterized earlier nomadic communities impossible. The birth of Athenian democracy reflected the increasingly egalitarian balance of property in the city. With economic growth, the need for legal services rose, initially through communal judging, since nobody could yet trust the judgment of individual judges sitting alone. These judicial assemblies later became legislative assemblies, and it was only then that the community actually created laws and a legal regime. For a full illustration of the rise of the law in ancient commercial society, Smith then used the example of Rome, which he regarded as another member of the family of ancient republics.

Smith shared with Rousseau a fascination with Rome. The second *Discourse* started with Rousseau comparing Rome to Geneva and with an agenda for how his modern republic must correct Rome's mistakes. This picture was later developed fully in *The Social Contract*. I shall come back to some of these points later, although I am afraid that I might suffer the same fate as Rousseau in Dijon, in his attempt to win the prize of the Academy in 1755 with his *Discourse on the Origin of Inequality*. The practice of the provincial academicians was to read out one prize essay each afternoon and judge it. The reading of Rousseau's masterpiece was abandoned midway, even before it could be condemned or praised. It was simply too long for oral comprehension and was hence deemed inappropriate for the occasion.

There are many reasons why, in the end, Rousseau's and Smith's politics come out differently while still standing in close proximity to each other. One reason is that Rousseau was Genevan, and *The Social Contract* addresses city republics like Geneva. Here the long-term history of Europe could be cut short by making it appear as if the politics of

ancient city-states, and particularly that of the Roman Republic, could
be continued a millennium and a half later. For Smith, there was a huge
gulf between the histories of ancient and modern Europe, which belonged to two different political cycles. Modern European liberty could
not be imagined easily as the continuation of ancient city-state liberty
because between them were the destruction of the Roman Empire, the
complete change of Europe's population, and the rise and subsequent
dissolution of feudalism. Although there were links back to Rome,
modern European politics was no longer the politics of city-states. To
explain the rule of law under these circumstances, one had to explain
both the dissolution of feudalism and the subsequent rise of modern legality, which took place in countries like England. Smith's history was
in this sense a real history of Europe. Rousseau's, at least in the second
Discourse, was much more a neo-Aristotelian history of changing forms
of government shifting under the impact of a single institutional development, namely the rise of inequality. Rousseau's history was a logical, not a historical, demonstration. As he explained:

> To understand the necessity of this progress one has to consider
> not so much the motives for the establishment of the Body Politic,
> as the form it assumes in its implementation, and the inconveniences
> it entails: for the same vices that make social institutions neces-
> sary make their abuse inevitable.[19]

If the state was established to protect private property, it could never
escape from this predicament. What Rousseau demonstrated was that
the dynamics of property relationships were disruptive and that the nature of commercial society made it very difficult, if not impossible, to
escape from its psychological effects. It was not just utility but the
combination of utility and recognition seeking that fueled the modern
economic machine. To control it, both utility and recognition seeking—
that is, *amour-propre*—would have to be controlled. Rousseau wanted
to show that Montesquieu's expectations for political and psychodynamic
equilibrium were no more than pious hopes because monarchies were
based on inequality and on formalized hierarchies of esteem and self-
esteem. These factors could not be eliminated from them. Indeed, Montesquieu's hope was that it was precisely this feature of monarchies, their

19. Rousseau, "Second Discourse," p. 182.

system of honor and false honor, that would provide the possibility of internal control. This is why Montesquieu's critics emphasized that a more egalitarian system was necessary to ensure France's survival and that the honor system had to be reformed accordingly. In their view, Rousseau demonstrated convincingly the impossibility of repairing France's ills if the wrong fusion of utility and pride were allowed to continue.

Smith insisted, like Rousseau, that utility and *amour-propre* had to be treated as connected and essential features of modern society, but in Smith's view, utility and authority could be connected differently, based on an alternative history of government and law than what Rousseau presented. For Smith, the problem with Rousseau was not so much the Hobbesian leanings, because Smith accepted the doctrine of sovereignty just as Rousseau did, but Rousseau's reliance on Locke in countering certain aspects of Hobbes's political advocacy. The way that Rousseau connected the history of property and the history of government had strong Lockean features. Locke had opposed Hobbes's absolutism and Filmer's paternalism. Rousseau continued with this historical pattern, whereas Smith decided that it needed to be overhauled completely. Smith learned from Hume that Locke's and Algernon Sydney's contractual theories of authority had to be rejected. Rousseau was traveling along parallel tracks but was heading the opposite way.

For Smith, the issue about the disputed priority of judges and the law was not new. A conspicuous feature of Locke's politics was that he had defined the state of nature as a condition without judges. He had also famously stated that history could never be a true source of normativity, for the past cannot bind the present or the future. Nonetheless, in order to rebut Filmer's absolutism, Locke developed his own history of early government in Chapter 8 of the second *Treatise*, "Of the Beginning of Political Societies," which immediately follows the much better known Chapter 7, "Of Political and Civil Society," the chapter that was the immediate target of Hume's and Smith's anti-contractual critique. In Chapter 8, Locke describes government as arising without any express and legally articulated consent. The state of nature was a social condition without institutionalized and centralized forms of judgment. Rather, each individual possessed an executive right of punishment, although as Locke emphasized, single individuals had the greatest practical difficulty in exacting such punishment. Actual punishment in the early stages of mankind was communally enacted justice of a nascent kind.

The formation of government could therefore be depicted as the slow emergence of communal judicial power. Locke's conjectural history of governmental authority was grounded on the idea that although human beings were jurally and normatively equal, they were conspicuously unequal in both physical and mental ability. It was these natural inequalities, on top of elementary differences in age and experience, that facilitated the emergence of leadership in early societies. Natural authority, Locke explained, led to executive power of a weak sort. Fathers of extended families continued in their leadership role even after their strictly parental function had ceased. Later, as larger social units were formed, these fathers became chieftains of tribes and eventually of the federation of tribes, called nations. How did judges emerge in these circumstances? As Locke pointed out, communities were threatened much more from the outside, by other communities, than by the domestic criminality of individuals. Hence the idea of leadership, the rule of man over man, first originated from attempts to deal with issues of external security, because this necessitated the creation of military command. Judicial power could be created more easily once military leadership had already been established. Judging, or judicial power, became an additional function of military chiefs. At first their offices were elective, but they were often transformed into hereditary positions over time. All these developments could easily be construed as consent based, for they were not forced on the population by anything other than difficult circumstances. Leadership arrangements were accepted voluntarily, for they answered a common need and were instruments of public utility, of the *salus populi*. Rule by natural authority, Locke emphasized, was based on naive trust and unguarded ignorance of the looming danger of cumulative and eventually irreversible corruption. The corruption of early governments could be reversed only through active resistance and revolution. This was achieved through the creation of legislative power. For Locke, corruption was inevitable because it was the effect of economic development. Natural authority and naive unconditional trust were feasible only while social and economic life was simple and relatively nonconflictual. Once money was invented, wealth accumulated and property rights proliferated, so the incidence of social conflict increased dramatically. With it grew the opportunity for abusing power. This part of Locke's history of government in the *Two Treatises* was exceedingly sketchy, as he simply hinted at the causal mechanism that was in play: fallen men were inherently corruptible, and their tendency for corruption was further aided and abetted by the rise of private property, which multiplied the opportunities for possessiveness and injustice. There were no inbuilt natural defenses in human nature against the rot of economic progress The invention of money broke all the natural limits of primitive society. This kind of corruption could be rolled back only by criminalizing and punishing political excesses through publicly stated and incontestable laws that were applied to rulers and the ruled alike. The invention of this kind of legislation required the establishment of a new kind of regime based on consent, in which the legislative body was supreme and was assigned the task of controlling corruption. In his second *Discourse*, Rousseau took over elements of both this story and Locke's theory of property and money, although he eventually developed them independently of Locke.[20]

Smith went down a different route. His theoretical history of law and government is both complex and detailed, traversing the entirety of European socio-legal development. Its shape, however, emerges quite clearly if we compare it to those of both Locke and Rousseau. First, his starting point was also a history of natural authority. Second, it is clear that Smith made a determined effort to relate the development of both law and government to economic development. Locke asserted that inequality and money undermined good government, which meant that the establishment of a fully legalized political regime was required to resist their corrosive effect. Smith had to fill the enormous gap that Locke left between his history of early governments and the modern English constitutional crisis. Further, since Locke had suggested that it was the rise of the economy that eventually corrupted government, Smith had to find an answer to this particular hypothesis. The result was the famous theory that commerce had not undermined but actually created liberty and legality. In this sense, Smith's answer to Locke also answered Rousseau. I shall consider its chief features in the second half of the book.

20. Hont discusses Locke's history of the emergence of governmental authority in "Adam Smith's History of Law and Government," pp. 142–45.

~ 4

Histories of Government: Republics, Inequality, and Revolution?

$\mathcal{I}$ FINISHED CHAPTER 3 by describing the rather surprising fact that Rousseau had read Locke quite carefully and had borrowed from Locke in such a way that he ended up arguing at cross-purposes with Smith. We are usually taught that Locke's politics had little influence in the eighteenth century and even less outside Britain. But in Rousseau, we can see a definite reception and impact. Hume argued that Locke's contract theory made little, if any, impression in Europe, and of course Locke himself argued in a similar fashion that Filmer's ideas were unheard of in Europe before he wrote. Rousseau, however, emphasized his opposition to Filmer's patriarchal politics and, in invoking Locke and Sidney against Filmer, also invoked the two names which Hume and Smith associated with the rise of vulgar Whiggism and party ideology in England. In some ways, Rousseau imported certain elements of the seventeenth-century English debate into the European political discourse of the mid-eighteenth century. Today we are taught to see Locke as an opponent of Hobbes and someone whose theory of political obligation can be regarded as valid only if it is understood as grounded in a fundamentally Christian political ontology. It is not clear at all that Rousseau would have realized the incompatibility between running Hobbes's and Locke's ideas together. Rousseau was not a resistance theorist, so the theological grounding of resistance rights in Locke probably did not matter that much to him.

In any case, one can see a number of reasons why Rousseau wanted to reject paternalist politics out of hand. His main borrowing from Locke was in property theory. He borrowed the labor-mixing theory of property from Locke, a doctrine which Hume and Smith rejected as technical chicanery, a clever substitution of the Roman law of accession for the standard theory of acquiring property by first occupation. First-occupation theories were indeed flawed, but Locke's substitution of the labor-mixing theory of ownership was no solution either. Nonetheless, it helped Rousseau a great deal in sequencing his history and theory of the first rise of government. It allowed him to argue that property was created first, and government, by contract, second. Later I will discuss aspects of this Rousseauian idiom as it relates to issues of political economy. What is of interest to me here is the deployment of the property first, government second, sequence for Rousseau's central purposes.

This order of sequencing was in many ways the standard order in the natural jurisprudence tradition, and Rousseau relied on Pufendorf in this respect, as well as on Locke. Smith, however, broke with this tradition. We possess two sets of student notes from Smith's natural jurisprudence lectures given at the University of Glasgow in the early 1760s. Their contents are nearly identical, and they still visibly follow the structure of the natural jurisprudence teaching that Smith had inherited from his two predecessors, Gershom Carmichael and Francis Hutcheson, who both used Pufendorf as their Urtext. But closer inspection shows that the two sets of lectures followed a different arrangement in one crucial respect. In 1763–1764, in the last year that he gave the lecture course, Smith revised the sequence of the core sections of his course. Instead of considering the nature and origin of property rights first, followed by an investigation of the jurisprudence of the family, and finally arriving at politics and the problems of government, Smith first explored the origins of government and only then moved to the question of property. He explained that he had wished to go back from the idiom of modern natural jurisprudence to the sequencing order of Roman civil law, from Pufendorf to Justinian. As Smith put it in his lecture:

> The civilians begin with considering government and then treat of property and other rights. Others who have written on this subject begin with the latter and then consider family and civil government. There are several advantages peculiar to each of

these methods, tho' that of the civil law seems upon the whole preferable.[1]

Sequencing the natural jurisprudential discourse is only one aspect of its explanatory content. Rousseau, for example, sequenced his history of law not as property-family-state, the purely logical sequence one finds in textbooks, but as family-property-state; and these things do matter. His sequencing problem related to his difficulty with Hobbes's idea that property and the state have to be imagined as having been created together. This idiom had to be deconstructed if Rousseau wanted to undermine Montesquieu's theory of the modern monarchy, which, as I explained earlier, was the purpose of the *Discourse on the Origin of Inequality*. Both Rousseau and Smith were theorists of the republic, the lawful state, or *res publica*. And, by a republic they did not simply mean collective government, or government by committee, but any form of government—by the one, the few, or the many—provided that it was a government of laws and not of men. Rousseau emphasized carefully in *The Social Contract* that the *civitas*, or city, could be monarchical, provided it remained firmly a *res publica*. Equally, Smith occasionally talked about monarchical republics, as most of his contemporaries did. Montesquieu's distinction between republics and monarchies, as two types of the *res publica*, was based on a somewhat different classification. For him, monarchy meant more than a lawful regime ruled by one person. He defined it as a *res publica* based on inequality. Rousseau's aim was to destroy this notion of *res publica* and to prove that states based on inequality were necessarily going to develop into despotisms and cease to be republics even if they started out as republics or even democracies. Rousseau's aim was to expose what in the nineteenth century came to be called the social question, the damaging tension within any state between legal equality and socioeconomic inequality. Rousseau criticized what he called the masterpiece of politics of the eighteenth century— that is, the idea that social cohesion, or at least a stable social order, could be created from the action of selfish agents who pursue their own interests, which, by virtue of this and without intending it, nonetheless serves the common good. The most famous assertion of this "masterpiece of politics" in Rousseau's epoch was Montesquieu's theory of

1. Smith, *Lectures on Jurisprudence*, p. 401.

modern monarchy. Such a system, Rousseau claimed, could not at the end remain compatible with the rule of law. Socioeconomic inequality was bound to destabilize the authority—that is, the legitimacy—of the *res publica*.

In Part I of the second *Discourse*, Rousseau turned Hobbes's theoretical notion of the state of nature into a conjectural history of the early stages of mankind's development. His history of government in Part II of the same work, however, was not historical even in this rather weak sense. There, he provided a developmental model of corruption from one form of government to another. His baseline was that lawful government could be formed only through a legal contract of all individuals within the state, equally and voluntarily. Subsequently, he demonstrated that if the contracting parties were economically unequal, their legal equality would also be destroyed. It is difficult to give a very succinct summary of Rousseau's main line of argument concerning the birth of inequality because he wove together several conjectural histories, such as the history of *amour-propre* and language, which was essentially not an economically based history, and the history of economic cooperation under northern climes, which was essentially a conjectural history of luxury. (Although I hasten to add that we should note that in the main text of the second *Discourse*—that is, the text without footnotes—Rousseau avoids the use of the term "luxury" like the plague. In fact, the word "luxury" does not occur in the main text once.) Rousseau assumed that people became irritated with one another once the rise of their comparative self-esteem had turned them into psychological competitors in the game of recognition. Justice and punishment became necessary, but before the birth of the law, there could not be judges; thus, individuals dispensed punishment as they saw fit, or as their physique and courage allowed them. This state of affairs could last only as long as individuals were separate social units. Once a society of economic cooperation arose and people lost their ability for self-sufficiency, legal individualism had to go the way economic individualism had gone. Both systems had to be socialized. Again, Rousseau pursued two lines of argument. One was about the rise of new needs, which was partly the story of *amour-propre* again, now in its role as a spur to economic development, which I will discuss in Chapters 5 and 6 in the context of political economy. Another line of argument, a semi-legal, semi-economic discourse, was about the transformation of long possession of land into property in land. This transformation led to a sharp rise of inequality, which led to an increasing tendency to conflict and violence and hence to a state of war or anarchy. Escape from this anarchy dictated the need for legality. *Cui bono?* asked Rousseau: Whose interest was served most by this? That of the rich, of course, who duped the poor into believing that the suppression of violence was in their interest too.

The poor were sold on the advantages of legal equality, which were quite real, without understanding the consequences of superimposing it on a system of unregulated private property. The most important point in this story for Rousseau's theoretical history of government in the second *Discourse* was to dismiss the notion that in the anarchy that prevailed before government was set up, this could be usefully conceptualized as the domination of the strong over the weak. That, he argued, was true in all situations of lawlessness. Rather, the anarchy preceding government had to be characterized as a conflict between two fundamental social classes, the "rich" and the "poor." Rousseau's point, which was about the type of social contract that concerned only legality, not property, was that it preserved the existence of these two classes as a founding feature of early governments. What the form of the early government became depended on the prevailing social configuration, on natural authority. Leadership figures, Rousseau assumed, were chosen because the people hoped to derive a benefit from their services. As a law of social dynamics, he assumed, just as Locke had done in his natural history of authority, that the leaders, magistrates, and generals would use their positions to their own economic advantage and that in due time would make their position a lasting one—that is, hereditary. Officeholders created and perpetuated sociopolitical inequality. The people accepted hierarchy because they hoped to slot in, but not at the lowest rung. They accepted masters so that they could be masters of others.

From this point on, Rousseau overtly tracked the birth of Montesquieu's monarchy as a system of inequality governed by the principle of false honor, a system fed by a rampant culture of *amour-propre* that eventually translated every inequality into an economic one, which, in turn, could be expressed as a difference in status measured by wealth and luxury. In his highly rhetorical language, Rousseau lumped together the eighteenth-century corruption of states, the rise of standing armies, the state as based on a balance or on a mixed government among the various estates, imperialism, luxury, and empty politesse. In other words, he described how monarchy was bound to become gradually more and more despotic by an incremental transformation of its principles of government from honor and false honor into fear and apathy. This, as Montesquieu himself had emphasized when describing despotism, was bound to lead to a kind of equality in fear, powerlessness, and moral degradation. States like this, Rousseau predicted, would suffer violent resistance and revolution at the end, which might restart the cycle of the developing tension between legal status, the form of government, and underlying social inequality, fueled by a culture of competitive recognition seeking.

Rousseau finished the second *Discourse* with a cultural but also political point about *amour-propre*. To the annoyance of the partisans of virtue, Rousseau steadfastly maintained that a corrupted people cannot be reformed in a lasting fashion. Unless the principle, the culture, and the underlying economic system of inequality changed, the members of the reformed state would still lack the psychological ability to transform their socially formed selves. A creature formed pathologically by a society cannot stand outside that society, but is bound to reproduce its essential features in a dialectic of recurrence. For Rousseau, revolution was a deeply futile and damaging phenomenon; not a rebirth, but a relapse.

Rousseau's *Social Contract* showed how this culture could be escaped if the establishment of legality by contract was not based on class war between rich and poor but if the rule of law was grounded in a moderately egalitarian socioeconomic formation. This state could be governed even monarchically and definitely did not need to be democratic, but it could not be a monarchy in Montesquieu's sense—that is, based on inequality and the culture of honor and false honor. This book was as much based on Montesquieu as was the second *Discourse:* it was an attempted repair and exposition of Montesquieu's idea that the principle of republics was patriotism or the love of country, which implied a suppression of the self—or, more precisely, of the selfish self. This quasi-Augustinian statement caused offense in the eighteenth century. Just as the subjects of monarchies could not accept that they lacked virtue, so the citizens of republics resented their exclusion from earthly happiness. This notion of the suppression of the self implied the view that the human self was not naturally prepared for being republican. Rousseau, like

Montesquieu, was an optimist in the old sense—that is, he accepted human nature as it is, as the best or optimal we can have and as not capable of essential improvement. In fact, this is the meaning of the statement at the beginning of *The Social Contract* that it takes men as they are. The point that Rousseau was making was that Montesquieu had not properly worked out how people can suppress their selves in a lasting fashion (the point of the "Tale of the Troglodytes" was that people would in the end get fed up with suppressing their selves and choose Montesquieu's monarchy instead). Montesquieu's model of republican culture was too individualistic, and Rousseau set out to show that a republican culture must be capable of producing a collective force for controlling individual selves through a *moi commun*, a collective "I." This was the idea that led him back to Hobbes, to the idea of the corporate state person, the people as a *moi commun* instead of just a multitude. Since the point was to avoid the history of government described in the second *Discourse*, the creation of stage two, that of a magistracy, which leads to monarchy, had to be blocked. Executive power as government could exist on a short leash, but legislative power, sovereignty, could not be alienated.

That is why *The Social Contract* can be described as trying to reinvent Hobbes's state without Hobbes's idea of representative sovereignty. Rousseau faced a hard task here. He could not use concord theory, because as Hobbes had shown, this necessitated a theory of prepolitical or natural sociability, and such a theory Rousseau did not have. So how did he create a theory of union without Hobbes's idea that it could only be done through a legal theory of representation? All the weight in Rousseau had fallen on culture, on the possibility, as Montesquieu had already suggested, of suppressing or harnessing *amour-propre* successfully through a collectivity—by individuals, but in company, as a people not a multitude. This required not only a new theory of representation without a unifier and without alienation of sovereignty but also an economic theory that could supplant luxury. The Physiocrats, once they had a chance to read *The Social Contract*, thought that Rousseau was a fellow traveler, a sort of honorary Physiocrat, and the Marquis de Mirabeau, Physiocracy's cofounder, wrote to congratulate the Genevan on his good taste in political theory. Rousseau was indignant. The legal despotism of the Physiocrats—that is, despotism on behalf of the laws and only the laws—was not an idea he could share. They were dreaming of a pure rule of law, a fully realized regime of laws, not of men. This,

Rousseau commented, was like dreaming of squaring the circle. It was bound to fail a priori. To appoint a very special kind of legal despot to personalize the pure rule of law was also a mistake, a conceptual contradiction. The ruler was bound to be a child of Adam, a fallen man, inevitably equipped with the sort of self that needed to be suppressed. But giving power to somebody was not the best way to suppress his fallen self. Power always corrupted, and absolute power corrupted even more. The self of the *moi commun* was a pure bundle of legality, to which Rousseau gave the name the general will. Except that the general will was not a person and was therefore not really a human *moi*. Rousseau was at a loss to find a proper linguistic expression to describe what he had in mind. It seems that he did not quite succeed in explaining himself clearly. And, of course, we still do not have the language to do so. State theory is still in a muddle. This, however, is not the time and place to pursue this particular issue. Rather, I will now turn my attention to Smith to develop the next stage of my comparative perspective.[2]

Montesquieu was an intensely historical theorist. Rousseau responded to Montesquieu as if the Bordeaux aristocrat were an analytical theorist in the Hobbesian mold. Smith didn't. He learned from Montesquieu that pure natural jurisprudence, analytical political-legal theory, had to be supplanted by an investigation of why these pure models had never been realized, through studying the distortions real circumstances can cause in political evolution. Smith's history, however, had a politically different hue. For Montesquieu, writing political theory as history meant a way of preventing revolution (the Germans took over his idea when they "invented" *Historismus*). Rousseau and Smith shared the same loathing of revolution and revolutionaries as Montesquieu, but they rejected his French solution to the problem of the nobility and the legacy of feudalism. They either ignored it or dismissed it. In fact, their contemporaries and immediate successors turned to their theories for advice precisely for this reason, because they were not obsessed with the nobility. This means that Smith wrote a history of law and government that was focused on republics, in the more capacious sense, both ancient and modern. By writing a history of *rei publicae*, he carried out a

2. Hont discusses Rousseau's theory of sovereignty in "The Permanent Crisis of a Divided Mankind: 'Nation-State' and 'Nationalism' in Historical Perspective," in *Jealousy of Trade*, pp. 469–74.

similar historicizing job on Rousseau as Rousseau had carried out on Hobbes's state of nature theory. Smith supplanted Rousseau's theoretical discourse of government with a historical one—or, more precisely, with a theoretical history. This resulted in a tripartite history. Like Rousseau, Smith had a history of the early stages of mankind undergirded by a stages theory of history, and then a history of political and legal liberty, or a history of republics *(rei publicae)*, in two parts. This latter topic had two parts because it was divided into ancient and modern history, just like the Oxford history curriculum. The ancient history part comprised the rise and loss of liberty and legality in Greece and Rome, and their subsequent physical and moral destruction by the German tribes in Western Europe. Then came the modern part, in which Smith developed his history of modern liberty, the kind of liberty that had ultimately been regained after the fall of Rome and the subsequent dark ages. Smith here used his reading of Montesquieu effectively, although not for the same political purpose as his French predecessor had intended. Modern Europe, as Montesquieu had already claimed decisively, was not a continuation of the ancients, nor was it just a simple revival or re-creation of ancient liberty in the wake of the Renaissance. The Italian republics, for Montesquieu as for Smith, were only a sideshow in European history. Smith thought that modern liberty was created or regained first and foremost in England, and he did not believe for a moment that England's much-vaunted modern legal regime could have been an offshoot of Florence, or a re-creation of Rome (in the way that this latter idea could be applied relatively plausibly to Geneva, for example). Rather, he had to write a complex history of how the modern republicanism of Europe was created in its large monarchical states. Modern liberty had a connection back to the ancients all right, but the connection in question was a tricky one, which had to be figured out.

Smith's work, like Rousseau's, remained fragmentary in the end. But just as Rousseau's work can be reconstructed from the two *Discourses*, the article on political economy in Diderot's *Encyclopédie*, the *Essay on the Origin of Languages*, the Geneva manuscripts of the book on political institutions, *The Social Contract*, the essay on Corsica, the pamphlet on Poland, and other materials, Smith's projected theory and history of law and government can be reconstructed from the student notes of his Glasgow jurisprudence lectures, his various essays, and his two major published works: *The Theory of Moral Sentiments* and *The Wealth of Nations*. When Smith later claimed that he had used some of this material in *The Wealth of Nations*, it was assumed that he meant the political economy part of his Glasgow lectures. In fact, what he meant was that half of his planned book was published in *The Wealth of Nations* as its Book III. It is easily recognizable what sort of history the third book was if we consider that a plagiarized adaptation of an earlier version of Smith's section became the introduction (written last, of course, as all introductions are) to William Robertson's *History of the Reign of the Emperor Charles V* as a theoretical history of modern European absolutism. The first part of the tripartite history appeared in Book V. The part dealing with the ancients remained unpublished, and that is why there was a persistent rumor until Smith's death that he would publish a history and theory of ancient government. This bit can indeed be reconstructed from his lecture notes. All three can be inspected together in the printed syllabi and lecture notes taken from John Millar's Glasgow lectures on government, which were a straightforward reprise of Smith's book in lecture form. In fact, Millar eventually published the first part of the tripartite structure as a book, *The Origin of the Distinction of Ranks*. One does not have to be a particularly adept speaker of eighteenth-century prose to recognize a translation of Rousseau into Montesquieuan dialect. *The Origin of the Distinction of Ranks* was Millar's—and, of course, originally Smith's—discourse on the origin of inequality and whether it was ever legitimized by natural law. I don't believe that Millar's was a plagiarism in the sense that Robertson's was, but how this semi-authorized version came about we do not know: Millar's papers were destroyed by his family. Whether Millar knew how much of Smith's lectures would resurface in *The Wealth of Nations*, we do not know either.

The similarities are obvious, but it is very rare that comments about it surface. In any case, it is clear that Smith was not writing a history of property but a history of political authority as a history of inequality. The connections to Montesquieu's theory of monarchy and to Rousseau's republican attack on Montesquieu are clear. It is a mistake to believe that the great discovery in the eighteenth century was republicanism. No, the exciting thing in the eighteenth century was the modern monarchy as a *res publica*. Today we talk about the age of democratic revolutions and the modern representative republic, our modern state form, as its product. In eighteenth-century conceptual vocabulary, the modern republic was of course the modern monarchy. The danger—clearly declared by Adam Ferguson, Montesquieu's closest critic and follower in the Scottish Enlightenment—was that fanatics of republicanism would mistake the modern republican monarchy for an ancient republic and try to suppress its modern element.[3] Blocking this possibility was already a major part of Smith's intellectual strategy in his history and theory of law and government. Montesquieu had already argued this in the case of Rome. Had Rome followed in its state form the monarchical transformation of its economic base (monarchical in Montesquieu's sense of a developing commercial society), the dangerous mongrel entity of a half-republican, half-monarchical state—that is, the principate or the empire—could have been avoided. Montesquieu's book *Considerations on the Causes of the Greatness of the Romans and Their Decline* was a key text here. This was the original trailer to *The Spirit of Laws*, and it is now often forgotten that in 1748, Montesquieu republished it as the companion volume to *The Spirit of Laws*, suggesting that the two books had to be read together (and they were read together; Thomas Nugent in England translated both). In fact, Montesquieu wanted to fold his unpublished 1735 pamphlet on universal empire into it, but this plan was aborted yet again by events in French politics, namely the messy end of the War of the Austrian Succession, presaging the Seven Years' War, which proved to be disastrous for French dreams of grandeur. It was from this quarter that Smith's protohistorical materialism—if that's what it was—emerged, namely from Montesquieu's analysis of the origins of the spirit of conquest, which had to be replaced, or so Montesquieu argued, by the spirit of commerce.

As I have already said, Smith returned to Locke's noncontractual history of government as set out in Chapter 8 of the second *Treatise*, which explained how governments that emerged from natural authority were corrupted by the rise of commerce, necessitating the revolutionary establishment of a proper political regime with the legislative body controlling executive power. In this perspective, the regime starts with legislative constitutional acts and then develops the executive power of government within the limits established by the legislative sovereign.

3. Adam Ferguson, *History of the Progress and Termination of the Roman Republic*, 5 vols. (Edinburgh: Bell and Bradfute, 1799); Ferguson, *An Essay on the History of Civil Society*, ed. F. Oz-Salzberger (Cambridge: Cambridge University Press, 1995).

Smith wanted to return this discourse to its historical origins. In history that is not the history of revolutions, executive power emerged first, then judicial power; in other words, first judges and then legislative power, or laws. This was the reverse sequence from the one Rousseau used. Smith agreed that the hunting–gathering stage of society was the real state of nature: there were no laws and no government. Society emerged, however, not from the division of labor or from festivities of love, but from warfare and from the formation of tribal or national groups. There was justice as a principle in all individuals. When people were hurt, they had anger, resentment, and a desire for revenge, all natural sentiments that followed from the constitution of the individual psyche. Punishment was possible if one had enough physical force to exact it. In fact, punishment was communal—not through organized communal enactments of justice but through spontaneous eruption of popular or group anger. Punishment was by ambush and by the lynch mob. This meant that punishment was both terrible and infrequent. As the demand for justice and punishment increased, a sort of institution of judgeship emerged through natural authority. In this Humean story, some individuals had the ability to judge cases and to give authoritative advice. Figures of authority emerged as leaders, and the primary need for leadership was in war. The federal or executive power created military leaders, and the incipient judicial functions were loaded onto them. Thus, there were judges first, but the law—the abstract principle— would not come till later. Nor was there any kind of social contract. Again, as Smith pointed out, the genesis had a different sequence from that of a revolutionary restoration. The modern or later problem is how to tone down the use of power through legitimation, how authority can replace force. Originally, however, as Locke had already argued, there was first authority and the genesis of power; the capacity for organized enforcement came only much later. The trick was to explain how authority figures acquired stable sources of power. It was at this juncture that Smith introduced wealth, as the most important source of authority, into the equation. He argued that the possession of authority—military or judicial, medicinal or religious—was the origin of wealth, not the other way around. Authority was rooted in service to others, and services had to be paid for. The psychology of recognition also dictated that the authority figures should become visibly wealthy—that is, visible possessors of authority. Inequality in possessions was due first to a gifting process by customers to service providers, and not the result of violence.[4]

Inequality seriously emerged not when property in land was invented (this was a much later development) but at the beginning of the shepherding or pastoral stage of society. Property of animals was the real great step forward, and it was this that made amassing serious wealth possible. When this happened, the authority figures—chiefly military leaders—could use their wealth to great advantage. Smith argued not only that wealth was power but also that power as such—stable power, that is—came from wealth. Wealth created the ability to provide livelihoods for those who did not have it; in other words, wealth could create dependency, which was the real source of power. This merger of authority and power in the shepherd stage of history, Smith claimed, was the origin of the state. It was not contractual or based on equality. What is important to notice here is the depiction of the direction of the historical trend. Smith did not see the secular trend of history as ever-growing inequality. Rather, the state starts with a very great, a brutally great, level of inequality. In the modern world, the sort of inequality that characterized early empires and shepherd garrison states, Smith claimed, is unimaginable. Think of the pharaohs of Egypt or Genghis Khan. No, the secular trend has been the diminution of inequality. Smith famously argued in *The Wealth of Nations*, following Locke and Mandeville, that modern workers lived better than the emperors of the past or the tribal chiefs of Africa or America.[5] He asserted something similar about power in general. This was the key notion behind the idea that commerce created liberty. It could do that because commerce created more equality in wealth than there had been at the beginning of the accumulation of wealth. Smith, like Hume, was a through and through Harringtonian. They both believed that forms of government, or regime types, reflected the underlying distribution of economic power. Power followed property, but property became more equally distributed as human history progressed, rather than the other way around. The ancient city-states became the cradle of legality because they were

4. Hont discusses Smith's theory of wealth and authority in "Adam Smith's History of Law and Government," pp. 150–55.

5. Smith, *TMS*, IV.1.10; Locke, *Two Treatises on Government*, ed. P. Laslett (Cambridge: Cambridge University Press, 1960), "Second Treatise," chap. 5; Bernard Mandeville, *The Fable of the Bees*, vol. 1, ed. F. B. Kaye (Indianapolis: Liberty Fund, 1988), p. 366.

the first to break away from the shepherd pattern of life and the shepherd system of chieftaincy, with its grounding in great inequality. The rise of the law was the result of economic development. As a more complex economic way of life created more and more need for both judicial services and a system of proportionate and regularized punishment, replacing the communal provision of justice became more and more necessary. The rise of many individual judges, or of individual judges as such, called for control over their activities, and it was the need to manage this service that lay behind the idea of introducing the law and legislation. The law was the vehicle for retaining communal control over a disaggregated or widely distributed system of justice that was supplied by a plethora of individual agents of justice. If justice had depended simply on the good sense of each individual judge, no court system could have emerged. The regularization of judgmental activity, of this fearsome power of judgment, was behind the rise of the law, and this could happen only where there was a tremendous need for such services, and where the dependency relations created by inequality in wealth could not override the push toward regularization through the sheer exercise of power over authority. For a long time, Smith emphasized, the Greeks were involved in developing regular systems of communal justice. People would go to the meeting to prevent injustice, which could also redound on them. That was the origin of assemblies, not politics or ideological dreams of liberty as such. The possible military use of communal justice was always present; the political use, as it were, came only later. Clearly, for Smith, the ancient polis, or *civitas*, was an urban commercial society that needed judicial services and hence developed them. Democracy and law were not inventions of the moral imagination but perfectly logical and regular consequences of a highly specific and new way of urban life. This was, if you wish, an economic interpretation of the origins of Greek democracy.

It is easy to see where this was going. Liberty could again be on the rise in Europe once the material preconditions of the ancient system of the *Rechtsstaat*, or perhaps just *Recht*, had come to be reproduced. Once Europe had again reached the Athenian level of commercial civilization and urbanization, it could have the rule of law. This was, of course, civil liberty. The point to note, however, is that for Smith, even ancient liberty is civil liberty—the judicial protection of the individual from his fellows, from their actions and judgments. In this scheme, political liberty implied protection of the rights of the individual from the encroachments of the mighty and the powerful, who could use the state to pursue their interest. It is this corruption that Rousseau modeled so starkly in the second *Discourse*. How this restoration of commercial society and hence the law happened in Europe was described in Book III of *The Wealth of Nations*, which I will discuss in Chapter 5. First, however, I will deal with the fate of the ancient republics.

In a pure stages theory, the correct development was achieved by the ancients. From the modern point of view, one could object that ancient commercial society was a slave economy, and this would have implied giving a demonstration of how the rise of legality could do away with the slave system and replace it with a model based on the working citizen. Eventually this did happen, but not as part of a continuous, uninterrupted development. What every schoolboy knew then, and perhaps knows even now, was that the ancient world of Europe had perished, was physically exterminated, by the Gothic holocaust. Why did this happen? Actually, the first explanation—the macro explanation, as it were—was the easiest to deliver in terms of a stages theory. Greece and Rome were avant-garde developments, islands of progress in the sea of the shepherd world of Asia and Europe. Instead of converting the shepherds to their way of life, it was the shepherds who prevailed in the end. The shepherds were military people for whom development and growth meant acquisition by conquest. Ancient legality was exterminated by military power or by war. Smith saw this as a fascinating issue. Death came not simply through numerical or demographical imbalance, although this was a crucial factor. People swarmed out of Siberia at an alarming rate and pushed westward, eventually overwhelming Rome. Greece, and later Rome, were threatened by Eastern empires too, and the Eastern half of Rome finally succumbed to the Arabs and the Turks, to Muslim shepherd societies.

What interested Smith was the loss of military capability in commercial society, both in Greece and eventually in Rome. These people were rich, hence they became constant targets of attack, but wealth also gave them the fruits of development—that is, technological advantages and resources in general. Why couldn't they find a military solution to secure their survival? Smith saw here a systematic problem that still had relevance for the moderns. Commercial societies, he continued as he developed the logic of the thought, could survive only if they developed an appropriately commercial mode of defense and mode of warfare in general. He identified the key in the existence of professional standing armies. The problem of the republican armies of Greece and Rome was that their militias were shepherd armies (the militia was the shepherd mode of military society), which initially became superior because of the superiority of the Greek and Roman urban republican state over a less developed civilization. However, as economic development changed the structure of these societies, they should have changed their armies. Montesquieu had already argued this case in general terms. Smith extended this analysis specifically to the military organization of society. At first, economic development, the development of justice and the state, made the Greek and Roman militia superior to the armies of shepherd empires because militias based on equality were superior to militias based not only on inequality but on extreme inequality. But as commercial society developed further, it became more and more a society of inequality, and not of a shepherd kind of inequality but of a new kind of commercial inequality. This undermined the egalitarian foundations of the Greek and Roman militias. Economic development had made these states powerful through the creation of legality and equality, but economic development had undone them too, because by destroying equality, it undermined their capability for self-defense—unless they changed their mode of warfare to a commercial one, namely to the employment of a professional standing army. Clearly the message, put across not too subtly, was that the moderns must not repeat this mistake.

When discussing the loss of ancient liberty, Smith made liberal use of the discourse of Renaissance and seventeenth-century republicanism for his purposes. His sources, in other words, were Machiavelli and James Harrington. Drawing on Machiavelli's chapter in Part II of the *Discourses on Livy*, and on Harrington's refurbishment of it, Smith asserted that republics had two modes of solving their security problems.[6] They could become either defensive or conquering republics; in other words, republics or commonwealths for "preservation" or "increase." Athens was the archetype of the first, Rome of the second.

Machiavelli expressed a preference for states that grew in territory, such as Rome, over defensive ones, which for him was exemplified by the Etruscan federation. Smith showed that both the distinction and

---

6. Niccolo Machiavelli, *Discourses on Livy*, ed. H. C. Mansfield and N. Tarcov (Chicago: Chicago University Press, 1996), book 2, chaps. 1–4; James Harrington, *The Commonwealth of Oceana*, in *The Political Works of James Harrington*, ed. J. G. A. Pocock (Cambridge: Cambridge University Press, 1977), pp. 180–82, 273–78, 320–25.

the concomitant preference were futile. Both kinds of ancient states had disappeared, even if Roman decline took longer to run its course than had the demise of Greece. Smith's first concern was to show that a purely defensive republic was impossible primarily because of inevitable changes in military technology. The material origin of republics was grounded on the idea that a fortified city could withstand attacks from a shepherd army (there is no mention here of Locke's labor theory of the acquisition of property; it was not that kind of economic interpretation of history). Over time, however, the military initiative swung to the attackers, and fortifications lost their pivotal martial importance. More importantly, Smith explained repeatedly, there was an incompatibility between economic development and warfare. The republic, as a political formation with an urban core, was an advanced economic formation, encouraging the growth of the arts and commerce. These occupations made the population disinclined to wage war. Stopping economic development, however, was not an option for city-based republics. Sparta could do it, but Sparta was not really a commercial republic. Smith explained the longevity of ancient republics by their use of slavery. Economic development, commerce, and the arts were carried on by slaves. This made it possible to use the republican citizenry for militia warfare for a significantly longer period.

For Smith, there was no predestined reason for a republic to become defensive or conquering. As Machiavelli pointed out in his *Discourses on Livy*, the issue was decided by a choice between exclusive and inclusive citizenship-acquisition policies. Restrictive or exclusive policies of citizenship resulted in a defensive republic, inclusive policies in an expansive republic. Eventually, however, the fate of conquering republics was the same as their defensive counterparts. For Smith, Machiavelli's reason for preferring the Roman option—namely that expanding empires made the acquisition of wealth for public flourishing, for republican *grandezza*, much easier—was quite meaningless. This type of external acquisition of wealth was, for Smith, the characteristic of shepherd states. The transformations taking place in Rome's economic organization, however, were much deeper than growing rich on the spoils of conquest. As a result, the sort of military greatness that Rome pursued became just as incompatible with commerce and manufacturing as Greek military policy. As it was for Montesquieu, Smith's main interest in discussing the Roman principate was to investigate the repercussions of the conquest strategy to the internal political constitution of the republic.

Rome's destruction was postponed for centuries because of the success of its strategy of eliminating the security problem by preemptive warfare. Shepherd states were conquering states. Hence, the appropriate defense posture was to respond in kind and to become a conquering republic. The strategy of conquest created a huge military presence within the republic, but the political costs of such a military establishment were enormous. Its existence caused Rome to relapse into a pre-republican, essentially shepherd political form, namely military government. Smith described this as a transformation of republican politics by a conquest from within: the republic was conquered by its army. Rome became a half-monarchical, half-republican military government. Despite this political militarization, Smith explained, great differences remained between imperial Rome and Asiatic military governments. Rome was a post-republican military state that inherited, preserved, and indeed further developed the civil government of the republic. Its military despotism, its confused reversion to a type of Asiatic shepherd state, coexisted with a strict regime of republican civil laws. There was a combination of a domestic republican private sphere with a commercial and manufacturing base and a shepherd-military superstructure. This republican private sphere made Rome militarily vulnerable. Securing the state would have required a professional army based on the division of labor. The actual Roman solution, to outsource national defense to shepherd mercenary militias, was a disaster. It left Rome defenseless once the shepherds turned against their masters.

It was a central tenet of Renaissance republican discourse that it was luxury that destroyed Rome by undermining its civic character and military prowess. Clearly, this was a kind of economic interpretation of history. Did Smith subscribe to it? Yes, he did, but with qualifications. He mentions Rome's destruction by luxury explicitly in his *Lectures on Rhetoric and Belles Lettres*, when teaching his students that historical explanations must not regress indefinitely. One had to terminate historical explanations by providing them with a baseline whose validity was widely accepted. Since the idea that Rome had declined because of its luxury was generally treated as a seemingly incontestable truth, it was possible to use it as a baseline for explaining the demise of the republic. Smith could have argued that the thesis was false, but he did not. His explanation of the demise of ancient republics amounted to a version of the idea that it was luxury that undermined classical republican politics.

This is an important point and not only because it makes it possible to compare Rousseau and Smith on luxury. It is often argued that Smith's emphasis on the economic basis of politics came from the jurisprudential character of the four-stages theory. But his history of European law and government was not simply or even mainly jurisprudential. His economic explanations of the trajectory of the ancient republics followed the drift of the republican analysis of politics, including the emphasis on the consequences of luxury. If Smith came to conclusions about modern politics that flew in the face of conventional republican arguments, this was not simply because of a preference for jurisprudence over civic humanism. Rather, he turned republican political analysis into modern political science, just as much as he turned natural jurisprudence into theoretical history. Instead of separating the two, or replacing the one discourse with another, he combined them. The idea that wealth and luxury dominated politics and law was present in both. Smith forged a new modern republican idiom in which the two predecessor discourses reinforced each other. Although this idiom was not necessarily liberal in a modern sense, it conveyed the original meaning of the term.

This will become even clearer when one considers the modern part of Smith's history of European law and government. This is the better-known part, because it became Book III of *The Wealth of Nations*. The story here is different from the ancient one. After the Gothic shepherds overran Europe, they settled in the ex-provinces of the Roman Empire, in large territorial units that later became the medieval kingdoms. The Germans represented the politics of shepherds. Once they settled down in Europe, they created feudalism, a mongrel kind of polity that consisted of the superimposition of shepherd military government over a nascent agricultural stage, based on the permanent settlement of the population within well-delineated tribal or national borders. Feudal government was not based on a city but on a scattered population. In a dispersed community, a new system of political communication had to be invented. This was the origin of representation as a mode of conducting modern, as opposed to ancient, government.

When the German tribes destroyed the Roman military empire, no remnant of ancient political republicanism survived. When Smith talks about the importance of medieval towns in early modern European history, it is crucial to notice that he does not equate them politically with ancient city-states, nor does he assume that the logic and institutions of city-state politics could simply be transferred to the large territorial kingdoms that were the main scene of Europe's development. Smith knew the republican city-state legacy of the Renaissance perfectly well. Nonetheless, he insisted that the little republics of Renaissance Italy and a few other isolated republican developments in Europe, such as Switzerland and the Netherlands, were not the key to explaining the rise of modern liberty. In his view, these republics were isolated occurrences in feudal and early modern Europe. The republican city-states of Italy were a product of the country's feudal anarchy. The fortified cities that survived from the Roman Empire not only preserved their intramural civil liberty but also enjoyed a defensive military advantage over the feudal aristocracy, who resided in the anarchical countryside. Eventually the towns conquered the country around them, becoming little republics. When the nobility of the countryside moved into the city, an urban-centered political regime arose.

These city republics became famous and important for Europe's progress, not because of their politics, Smith argued, but because they amassed enormous wealth and became the economic leaders of Europe. They were, Smith claimed, at least two full centuries ahead of the rest of Europe in terms of economic development. This was the real base of their *grandezza*. Their wealth, however, was not simply the result of natural social and economic growth or of political advantage; it was an outcome of a confluence of causes. One was geography—the Mediterranean position of Italy, between East and West. Another was the enormous war profits that were gained from providing economic and logistical assistance to the Crusades, a unique ideological-military event whose causes stood outside any regular pattern of social and economic development.

Smith then applied his general theory of the decline of ancient republics to the Renaissance ones too. As they became rich and economically advanced, they were destined to decline militarily. Those who understood the history of the ancient republics wished to stop the development of manufacturing in their city-states, as Machiavelli's hero Castruccio Castracani had done in Lucca, but if they succeeded, they only rendered their own republic backward and insignificant. The rich and successful ones were weakened militarily by their luxury and commercial-manufacturing mode of living. The lack of slavery in modern republics implied that the general population had to be busy conducting the daily functions of economic life. Hence, Smith argued, there were no significant instances of democracy in Renaissance Italy. There were only aristocracies, because political participation by working artisans would have been very time-consuming. The same applied to the military. Yet again, military technology advanced, making the defense of walled cities and the conduct of modern warfare increasingly difficult. The republican militias were no match for the professional monarchical armies of Europe.

Eventually, Smith concluded, the small Italian city republics perished by war and declined into relative insignificance, just as their ancient predecessors had done. This meant that the rise of European liberty had to be explained in the context of the demise of the German shepherd politics of feudalism. Was there a revolution against feudalism? Was it conquered from outside, like the ancients and the Renaissance city-states? No. The feudal or post-feudal states were the conquerors in the Italian case. So, what had undone them? Smith's answer was partly the same as in the ancient case: luxury destroyed them. He also claimed that it was the same luxury that had destroyed Rome. It was in fact Roman luxury that had undone the feudal kingdoms. When dying, Rome bequeathed its poison to its conquerors. But this poisoned chalice of Roman luxury, transmitted through the surviving Roman towns, brought liberty back. It was this theory that made Smith so different from Rousseau in the end—or so it seemed to many readers. I shall discuss their political economy, that is to say their ideas on luxury, in Chapters 5 and 6. Rousseau knew the same Machiavelli passages very well. He also thought that the idea of a government for increase was a vicious one, one that had poisoned Europe. He was, of course, radically against it. But he also thought that the Hobbesian theory of the state as a corporate person was not immune to this disease. On the contrary, Rousseau thought that the artificial person of the state had an artificial appetite, without obvious physical limits. Controlling the economic appetite of the state did indeed become a major eighteenth-century problem. It will be interesting to see how Rousseau and Smith dealt with it.

~ 5

Political Economy: Markets, Households, and Invisible Hands

𝒥N THIS CHAPTER, I step into the realm of political economy, which, in practice, will turn out to be the territory of the luxury debate.

I argued that Smith accepted the thesis that it was luxury that destroyed the ancient republics, by destroying their military capacity. They could not defend themselves against the attack of shepherd nations, which were one rung—or perhaps even two rungs—down, in the four-stages scheme of history, from the agricultural-commercial societies that they destroyed.

Rousseau also accepted the truth of this thesis concerning the demise of the ancients, but he saw a paradoxical element in its origins. The thesis that luxury had destroyed ancient European civilization actually originated from the ancients themselves, who were capable of formulating the best theoretical accounts of their own demise. This was not an explanation after the event; it was a prediction that had come true. Whatever the problem with ancient societies, it was not their lack of theoretical understanding. Their problem was not actually with theory but with practice. While declaiming against luxury, the ancients had begun to practice it, and watched themselves sliding down its slippery slope. Ultimately they went down altogether, while still remaining fully aware of their mistake.

According to Rousseau, there were two possible responses to this spectacular mishap. One was to deny the validity of the ancient analysis of the political and national security consequences of luxury. Rousseau referred to two modern writers in this respect, probably Mandeville and Jean François Melon. These authors argued that luxury was not the bane but rather the basis of the well-being of societies and was entirely manageable if it was understood properly. Rousseau rejected this answer out of hand because he thought that it was perverse. The ancient failure was not because the theory was false but because the ancients did not follow their theory in practice. It followed that the task was to construct a society in which philosophers, politicians, and the people drew on the lessons of the ancient critique of luxury and then built a durable practice on it. Rousseau claimed that this was the purpose of his own political economy project.

It was this project that made Kant distinguish Rousseau from the Epicureans. The Epicureans, pursuing their idea of happiness, focused on need satisfaction as the primary vehicle for developing morality. They took the refinement of needs to be a progressive feature of human history. When Kant, following Cicero's *De Finibus*, presented ancient moral thought as a controversy between Stoics and Epicureans, he placed the Cynics on the Epicurean side of the equation. The Cynics, epitomized by Diogenes, were theoretical hedonists who saw morality as an instrument of happiness. However, they differed from the Epicureans on the question of luxury and artificial needs. They identified happiness with an ultra-minimalist program of needs satisfaction, virtually regarding the bare satisfaction of physical needs as the key to morality. This, Kant pointed out, was why their thought could be described as a shortcut to morality. The real difficulty, he added, was to combine morality with the difficulties caused by the culture of artificial needs that constituted civilization. He characterized Rousseau as hovering between this Cynic or Diogenean position and an Epicurean understanding of moral development. He called Rousseau a refined or subtle Diogenes.[1] This was a correct analysis. Rousseau himself positioned Diogenes in the same moral tradition that included Hobbes, and his own theory of *amour-propre* emphasized that it was one of the emotions that produced both the good and the bad in the history of humankind. Referring to the

1. Kant, "Moral Philosophy," p. 45.

famous story of the encounter between Alexander the Great and Dio-genes, Rousseau declared that *amour-propre* produced both the great warrior emperor and the exceedingly modest and proud philosopher. They grew, as it were, from the same ancient root.[2]

As we saw earlier, Smith was dubbed by his Scottish contemporaries as a refined or subtle Epicurean. What they meant was something sim-ilar to what Kant said of Rousseau, namely that he did not fully sub-scribe to a hedonist theory of luxury and artificial needs. It seems that Rousseau and Smith were somewhere in the middle of a moral and eco-nomic spectrum stretching from the minimalism of the ancient Cynics to the full hedonism and pro-luxury position of those who were dubbed Epicureans in the eighteenth and nineteenth centuries. The middle of the spectrum, of course, is still a large space, but in comparing the Ge-nevan and the Scot, one should not talk about two thinkers occupying polar positions but instead take them both as critics of the excesses of commercial society. We need to dissociate ourselves from the popular eighteenth-century image of Rousseau as a dogmatic Cynic—a true fol-lower of Diogenes, who wanted us to go all the way back to the level of elementary needs satisfaction. Rousseau explicitly denied this on many occasions.

My next step is to tackle head-on one of the most egregious misun-derstandings of the difference between Rousseau and Smith, which is their views on markets. I have in mind the famous idiom of the invis-ible hand. In itself, the metaphor of the invisible hand was quite trite. The hidden hand was meant to be God's, and it occurred in a great many sermons in the eighteenth century, derived from the argument about design. Rousseau used the metaphor casually in the notes to the second *Discourse*, when he described the remarkable physical abilities of savages, in this case the Hottentots, who played a throwing game with pebbles. They hit their target with such precision, Rousseau wrote, that it seemed as if the pebbles were guided in their flight by an invisible hand. Smith used the metaphor in *The Theory of Moral Sentiments*, in the context of defending private property from Rousseau.

This passage occurs in an analysis of *amour-propre*. Smith argued that artificial needs were not the result of chasing physical pleasures but arose

2. On Rousseau as a Cynic, see M. Sonenscher, *Sans-Culottes: An Eighteenth-Century Emblem in the French Revolution* (Princeton: Princeton University Press, 2008), pp. 134–201.

from the process of status seeking. To be poor was shameful and was why poor people wanted to become rich. Thereby they accepted the culture of the comparative self, of *amour-propre*. In the first half of the chapter, Smith's purpose was to show the circuitous ways the human imagination worked. The rich consumed luxury products not simply as symbols of status and power; they were also enchanted by the complicated construction of gadgets. He rehearsed Hume's point that at the higher levels of luxury, it was not the utility of these sorts of objects but the beauty of their design that pleased their owners. This analysis led to an evaluation of the entire civilization to which sophisticated and aesthetically mediated utility seeking belonged. Here Smith conceded Rousseau's case, also describing the hectic culture of status seeking as a giant deception. The next step of his analysis was a rudimentary theodicy. The deception, Smith argued, was for the benefit of mankind. Closely paraphrasing his own translation of Rousseau in the *Edinburgh Review*, he claimed that it was this deception

> which first prompted [people] to cultivate the ground, to build houses, to found cities and commonwealths, and to invent and improve all the sciences and arts, which ennoble and embellish human life; which have entirely changed the whole face of the globe, have turned the rude forests of nature into agreeable and fertile plains, and made the trackless and barren ocean a new fund of subsistence, and the great high road of communication to the different nations of the earth.[3]

The modern global economy originated in its entirety from this deception. The "invisible hand" passage followed this statement, challenging one element of this picture.

Rousseau had argued that private property, meaning fixed possession beyond personal need, allowed one person to possess as much as could meet the needs of two people or more. It was this move, Rousseau claimed, that created the slippery slope of corruption in modern civilization. Smith's answer was the same as the one Locke had given in the property chapter of the second *Treatise of Government*: that none of this mattered if productivity also doubled. More than this, the balance would

3. Smith, *TMS*, IV.1.10.

even turn positive if productivity outstripped the growth of selfish ac-quisitiveness. Smith, at this point, was intent to show that the alter-native that Rousseau was suggesting, egalitarianism, would not have worked any better, and that the inegalitarian solution of allowing pri-vate property to grow beyond personal needs had proved beneficial to mankind. The invisible hand was part of Smith's rhetoric in developing this point.

Nonetheless, Smith's tone was enormously hostile to private prop-erty owners, and toward landowners in particular, in this entire section of the book. The point Smith made was technical. A rich man could own a great deal of land, which yielded a huge amount of produce. But only in his imagination could he appropriate it all for himself. Physi-cally, this was plainly impossible. The body, the stomach of the rich man, was no larger than that of the poor man. The homely and vulgar proverb that the eye is larger than the belly, Smith wrote, was never more fully validated than with regard to the rich man. The rich man did not eat more than the poor. Rather, he had better and fancier meals. The rest of his property he sold on the market. His possessions were not natural; they had to be produced with the help of human labor. Since the rich man did not work, he had to hire others to make his property produc-tive. In addition, the rich were employing servants to service their needs. Thus, those who had no property other than their labor could work for the rich in one capacity or another and earn wages, and this in turn al-lowed them to eat, clothe themselves, and have families. This market system, or the exchange between the owners of property and the owners of labor, Smith claimed, worked at least as well as, and often better than, the egalitarian system. This was not a moral but an economic judgment. The luxury and misbehavior of the rich were not excused. But from a utilitarian point of view, mankind did benefit. As Smith wrote:

> The [rich] consume little more than the poor and in spite of their natural selfishness and rapacity, though they mean only their own conveniency, though the sole end which they propose from the la-bours of all the thousands whom they employ, be the gratification of their own vain and insatiable desires, they divide with the poor the produce of all their improvements.[4]

4. Ibid.

The corollary was as follows:

> They [the rich] are led by an invisible hand to make nearly the same
> distribution of the necessaries of life, which would have been made,
> had the earth been divided into equal portions among all its inhab-
> itants, and thus without intending it, without knowing it, advance
> the interest of the society, and afford means to the multiplication
> of the species.[5]

The interaction between the haves and the have-nots was not a zero-
sum game. "When Providence divided the earth among a few lordly
masters," Smith intoned, using or perhaps mocking the providentialist
idiom of Christian moral theorists, "it neither forgot nor abandoned
those who seemed to have been left out in the partition." Happiness
among men was far more broadly distributed: "These last [the proper-
tyless] too enjoy their share of all that [the earth] produces. In what con-
stitutes the real happiness of human life, they are in no respect inferior
to those who would seem so much above them."[6]
The mechanism that ensured this outcome was the discrepancy between the physical capacity of the human body and the flexibility of the
human imagination, between physical and artificial mental needs, or,
in other words, the tension between physical and moral man, *l'homme
physique* and *l'homme morale*. The interplay between these two aspects
of human identity was a major Rousseauian theme, perhaps *the* Rousseauian theme. Is it possible that Smith was adumbrating, in the "invisible hand" passage in *The Theory of Moral Sentiments*, a theme that
Rousseau could readily, even enthusiastically, agree to?
This is one of those important junctures where one needs to tread
carefully. Yes, Rousseau and Smith developed very different solutions
to the issue of private property. Smith put his finger here on one of the
central points of Rousseau's understanding of commercial society. But
no simplistic understanding of the opposition between the two thinkers
will serve us well here. The underlying explanatory point from which
Smith developed his own argument was perfectly acceptable to Rousseau. He expressed the same idea several times himself, both in pub-

5. Ibid.
6. Ibid.

lished form in *Emile* and in the various fragments of his abandoned masterwork, the "Institutions of Politics." Rousseau kept repeating the point that the rich were physically no different from the poor (if this were not so, what would happen to them when a revolution reversed the places of the two classes in the social hierarchy? Rousseau asked). It was not difficult to see that their physical consumption patterns did not differ widely, either.

The most interesting appearance of this thought occurred as part of Rousseau's refutation of the Hobbesian idea that the state of nature was a state of war between individuals. According to Hobbes, individuals develop insatiable desires, and without a state, they were bound to be at constant war with one another. Rousseau saw this primitive interpretation of insatiable human needs as highly problematic. How could anyone believe that the rich actually used up all the fruits of their vast property? What was the produce of property good for in itself, if not to be passed on to others?

> What good are even riches if not to be spent; of what use would the possession of the entire universe be to him if he were its sole inhabitant? What? Will his stomach devour all of the earth's fruit? Who will gather for him the produce from the four corners of the earth; who will carry the evidence of his empire to the vast wastes he will never inhabit? What will he do with his treasures, who will consume his provisions, before whose eyes will he display his power?[7]

The stomach of the rich, Rousseau nailed down his point, was no larger than anyone else's. Rousseau's argument was clearly a carbon copy of that of Smith:

> There is a limit to man's force and size, fixed by nature and which he cannot exceed. From whatever angle he looks at himself, he finds all of his faculties limited. His life is short, his years are numbered. His stomach does not grow with his wealth, regardless of how much his passions increase, his pleasures have their measure, his heart

7. Jean-Jacques Rousseau, "The State of War," in *The Social Contract and Other Later Political Writings*, ed. V. Gourevitch (Cambridge: Cambridge University Press, 1997), p. 165.

has bounds like everything else, his capacity for enjoyment is always the same. He may well aggrandize himself in idea, he remains ever small.[8]

Rousseau's general point was that *amour-propre* and pride were agents of sociability, thereby repeating Hobbes's point in *De Cive*. The comparative psychology of recognition presupposed society and only made sense in society: the proud self had to have interaction with others. The rich could not consume all the produce of their vast property. The strong and powerful could not murder all their competitors in war. Who would then admire their superiority? Who could serve them? Naive and moralistic interpretations of private property and inequality were completely unrealistic. Instead of murdering the enemy, Rousseau pointed out, one could make them slaves. Similarly, instead of excluding the poor from the fruits of property, one could make them market or wage slaves. The Marxian overtones of this idea are clear, but it was ninety years before Marx wrote his version.

Before discussing this issue further, we need to note the nature of the text from which I have been quoting. It was a fragment of the "Institutions of Politics," which has come to be called "The State of War" by posterity. Its central argument is that the real state of war in the modern world is not between individuals and social classes within individual states but between nations, in the domain of international anarchy. The real problem with insatiability and greed was not the behavior of individuals, propertied or otherwise, because the danger stemmed not from natural persons but from state persons. Rousseau here made full use of his theory of the state as a corporate person (probably Hobbesian, although the idea was also central to the article "State" in the *Encyclopédie*, published under the name of the Chevalier de Jaucourt). In comparison to the limitations of true human individuals, Rousseau wrote,

The State, by contrast, being an artificial body, has no determinate measure, it is without definite proper size, it can always increase it, it feels weak so long as some are stronger than it. Its security, its preservation demand that it make itself more powerful than all of its neighbours. It can only enlarge, feed, exercise its forces

8. Ibid., p. 168.

at their expense, and while it may not need to look for its subsistence outside itself, it does constantly look outside itself for new members who might give it greater stability. For the hands of nature set bounds to the inequality among men, but the inequality among societies can grow endlessly, until one absorbs all the others.[9]

The language of this passage is extremely close to Rousseau's language in his article on *Economie politique* in the *Encyclopédie*, where he also analyzed the need for states to grow. There, Rousseau openly rejected the famous passage in Machiavelli's *Discourses on Livy*, in which the Florentine expressed a strong preference for states that increased their wealth and glory continuously, by conquest if necessary.[10] Clearly the fragment, which is now in the Rousseau archive in Neuchâtel, further explicated the argument of the article on *Economie politique*. Rousseau was a consistent enemy of militarism and imperialism. In the fragment, he showed that he was an opponent of nationalism too. Nationalism was *amour-propre*, as applied not to natural but to state persons. States, Rousseau claimed, were driven by their *amour-propre* far more strongly than were natural persons, because their boundaries were so much more fluid and vague. The international power game was played by a much smaller number of actors than the membership of even the smallest of national societies. On the international level, recognition seeking was everything, and it was also brutally direct. The growth of any neighbor made other nations automatically look smaller in comparative terms, unless they responded. Artificial state persons were weak and shaky. National psychology had to be cultivated much more intensely than even the pathological psyches of individuals. The passions of nations were dangerous, and those of republics were the most dangerous of all.

"A thousand writers have dared to assert that the Body politic is without passions and that there is no other reason of state than reason itself," Rousseau wrote. And he continued as follows:

As if it were not evident that, on the contrary, the essence of society consists in the activities of its members, and that a State without movement would be nothing but a dead body. As if all of

9. Ibid., p. 169.
10. Machiavelli, *Discourses on Livy*, bk. 2, chap. 4.

the world's histories did not show us the best constituted societies also to be the most active, and the continual internal as well as external action and reaction of all their members did not bear witness to the entire body's vigour.[11]

Rousseau was absolutely clear about the consequences: "For this state to endure, the liveliness of its passions must therefore make up for the lack of liveliness of its movements, and its will must quicken by as much as its power grows slack."[12]

As states grew, their public spirit inevitably slackened. Revitalization required action, which tended to be expansionary, aggressive, and hostile to neighbors. In fact, the easiest way to preserve a state's economic greatness, a purely comparative or relative concept if ever there was one, was to impoverish its neighbors by putting obstacles in the path of their growth, even militarily, if necessary. This was Rousseau's version of Smith's damning analysis of the mercantile system, which, Smith claimed, was a form of economic policy that was based on both national animosity toward others and national aggrandizement domestically. Both Rousseau and Smith were agitated about Europe's predicament in the mercantile system and were looking for a remedy. I aim to talk about their proposed solutions in Chapter 6.

For now, however, I would like to return to the domestic problems of commercial societies. As we saw, the issue was not so much private property and its consequences in the misery of the excluded or propertyless class; the surpluses of the wealthy were distributed through markets. Instead, the problem was economic enslavement by means of the unjust operation of markets. I would like to call your attention to a little-noticed aspect of a very famous passage in Rousseau's *Discourse on the Origin of Inequality*. The passage I have in mind is the "fatal accident" of discovering metallurgy and agriculture.[13] The crucial point here relates to metallurgy. Rousseau's famous rant against private property at the beginning of Part II of the second *Discourse* concerned private property in land—in other words, in relation to agriculture. Metallurgy was different; it did not involve the invention of a new species of property.

11. Rousseau, "State of War," p. 169.
12. Ibid., p. 170.
13. Rousseau, "Second Discourse," p. 167.

It is often interpreted as a "fatal accident" because it led to an escalation in the spiraling growth of artificial needs that characterized the history of civilization under the influence of *amour-propre*. This is true, but there was an extra factor. Metallurgy gave rise to industry, a species of economic endeavor divorced from the land. A metallurgist did not produce food but exchanged his products for it. This was a huge step forward in the division of labor.

It was a huge step because it created two classes of laborers in society: those who produced food, and those who produced artifacts. The industrial class could only get access to food by exchanging their products for the produce of the agriculturalists. From this it follows that agriculture should have remained pivotal for the working of the entire system. The fatality of the invention of metallurgy, as Rousseau now explained, was that there was no proper balance between the two economic classes. Rousseau assumed that the terms of exchange between industry and agriculture were inherently lopsided. Industry was infinitely more dynamic by its very nature than agriculture: it was a novelty from the beginning, and it kept producing new items for which there was a demand or desire. As a result, the terms of trade between agriculture and industry were tilted against agriculture from the very beginning. Food was cheap; industrial products were expensive. This gave rise to a world where industry and the cities (or the places where industry was practiced) increasingly dominated agriculture and the rural population. This, Rousseau explained, was eventually bound to lead to a huge demographic crisis. The chief economic effect of the invention of metallurgy was this tragic imbalance in the modern economy, which could lead to social collapse and depopulation. This was the major fear that Rousseau expressed vividly in the notes to the second *Discourse*. This issue, of course, was a, if not *the*, major economic preoccupation of his age. It was very much the case in Switzerland but perhaps even more so in France, where the imbalance between industry and agriculture, city and countryside, was, apart from the subject of public debt, France's chief problem and the most damaging legacy of the age of Louis XIV and Colbert. It was also central to the work of Adam Smith. The simplest definition of the content of *The Wealth of Nations* is that it gave a counterintuitive answer to this issue. Smith acknowledged the existence of the problem of the imbalance between agriculture and industry and its huge importance. Nonetheless, he claimed that it must be solved not by redressing the imbalance between industry and agriculture by repressing industry, but by maintaining its leading role in society and even increasing it, provided that the terms of trade between industry and agriculture were revised. Agricultural products had to be allowed to rise in price, making the activity profitable and hence dynamic. Smith claimed that the imbalance observable in the eighteenth century between industry and agriculture was not simply a product of recent mistaken policy—it was constitutive of the history of the modern European economy. Europe had grown into the powerhouse of the world precisely through exploiting this imbalance, Smith explained. Rolling it back could endanger Europe's entire economy.

Even more importantly, Smith claimed that this imbalance had been a hugely important contributor to Europe's return to liberty after the feudal period. Remember, Smith associated liberty with the rise of legal regimes and claimed that legality was the natural product of urbanized commercial society. Europe became free after the feudal period because the towns and cities had led its economic recovery. As their economic weight grew, their legal culture grew mightily in importance. Rolling back the influence of cities, therefore, could endanger the entire post-feudal political edifice of Europe. To justify the claim, Smith needed to work out an answer that would allow him to have his cake and eat it too. He wanted the urban economy and urban liberty to remain dominant, but he also wanted agriculture to catch up, abolishing any imbalance and injustice in the fundamentals of the European economy. The second part of his history of law and government, the history of modern European liberty, was designed to solve this problem. This was the reason it became Book III of *The Wealth of Nations*.

What were Rousseau's thoughts on this issue? Clearly, it was of paramount importance for him. Interestingly, the word "luxury" does not appear in the main text of the *Discourse on the Origin of Inequality* that was submitted to the academy of Dijon. It appeared, however, in the note attached to the main text, precisely in the context of a discussion of the impending demographic catastrophe that the imbalance between city and country could cause. Luxury, Rousseau claimed, would lead to depopulation, the withering away of the strength of Europe. He knew that this trend had to be stopped, and by drastic means if necessary. But how could luxury be killed off? Rousseau ruled out any egalitarian experiments or any fantasies about natural abundance. An economy based on naturally unequal individuals could never be straightjacketed by egalitarian imperatives. He was not against private property as such, or against a transactional exchange society. He did not want a command economy, based on enforcement. Rousseau was essentially a kind of libertarian. He defined the economy as the mutual and just—that is, equal—exchange of labor. He wanted a situation in which agricultural and industrial labor were properly valued and exchanged on a fair basis, leading to just terms of trade between the two economic sectors. He wanted a society where everybody could get work and obtain what he or she needed in exchange for wages. Membership of a commercial society for Rousseau had to be through labor. This idea was clearly expressed in *Emile* and is clearly the origin of some of Emmanuel-Joseph Sieyès's ideas in his famous pamphlet *What Is the Third Estate?*, where the answer to the question of what social membership was to consist in was the Rousseauian one. Those who didn't work, Sieyès claimed, were not properly members of society and deserved no representation.[14] Rousseau didn't wish to exclude money as a means of exchange in a society constituted by and through labor. What he wanted to figure out was how to gain real control of the monetary processes in a society—in other words, how to understand, control, and reform price mechanisms. After all, his complaint was that agricultural prices did not express the real value of agricultural produce, that the terms of trade between industry and agriculture were systematically biased. Taking his cue from Richard Cantillon, the Irish banker whose work was published posthumously in 1755, Rousseau adopted the quantity theory of money, meaning that prices varied with the quantity of money in society.[15] Richer societies had more money and hence higher price levels. But the impact of historically high price levels on the various social classes differed a great deal, and Rousseau assumed that agricultural incomes necessarily lagged behind those of others. Agriculturalists and ordinary people, in other words, suffered from the high prices of modernity. The impact was visible as a demographic catastrophe, exacerbated by the higher mortality rates in cities dominated by luxury and unhealthy living conditions. Rousseau clearly wanted to redress the balance. The question was how.

14. Sieyès, "What Is the Third Estate?," pp. 94–95, 134.
15. Richard Cantillon, *Essai sur la nature du commerce en général*, ed. H. Higgs (London: Macmillan, 1931).

In order to understand this, one needs to understand Rousseau's underlying theory of balanced economic growth or, in fact, his theory of the balanced growth of human civilization as such. Clearly, this balance had to give rise to a just proportionality between town and country, industry and agriculture. But Rousseau's balance was a much deeper one because it was also related to the balanced nature of the entire civilizatory process. The goodness of natural or physical man (the two adjectives described the same phenomenon) was not a form of moral goodness. Remarks such as "Man is by nature good [*bon*]"[16] or "Whatever is, is right [*bien*] upon leaving the hands of the author of things"[17] are frequently taken to imply that in Rousseau's view, humans, at least at the beginning of history, were good in some sense, which could resonate with the evaluations and understanding of civilized man. Evil, in the theodicy that framed Rousseau's "sad"—that is, "optimist"—system (the terms were used counterintuitively by him, at least from the perspective of modern usage), mainly referred to physical evil and was used to describe those events that happened to individual humans or to the human species without them being able to do much about it. In his *Confessions*, Rousseau described himself as crying out in the *Discourse on the Origin of Inequality:* "Fools, who constantly complain about nature, learn that all your evils are due to yourselves."[18] This was also his guiding thought in *Émile*, which opened with the quintessentially optimist formula: "Whatever is, is right upon leaving the hands of the author of things: everything degenerates in the hands of man."[19] If, as Rousseau claimed, "our greatest evils come to us from ourselves," then political theory had to start from how men are, not how they could be. This was exactly the same claim that Rousseau made at the beginning of his *Social Contract*. Laws could be changed, but not man.

What did Rousseau mean by referring to Pope's phrase, "whatever is, is right" (which was translated as "good," *bien*, in French), in this context?[20] He was referring to the thesis that the first part of his *Dis-*

---

16. Rousseau, *Lettre à Christophe de Beaumont*, Œuvre complètes IV, ed. B. Gagnebin and M. Raymond (Paris: Gallimard, 1969), pp. 935–36.

17. Rousseau, *Émile*, bk. 1, OC 243, p. 161.

18. Rousseau, *Confessions*, bk. 8, OC I.389, p. 326.

19. Rousseau, *Émile*, bk. 1, OC 243, p. 161.

20. Alexander Pope, *An Essay on Man* [1733/34], *Poetical Works*, ed. Herbert Davis (Oxford: Oxford University Press, 1966), epistle I, 294; epistle IV, I, 394.

course on the Origin of Inequality was intended to debunk, namely the idea that man's weakness, his *imbecillitas*, was the root cause of society. There was no weakness in natural man; he was "good," Rousseau claimed. What disturbed the peace, and was the cause of evil, was the fact that man was a composite creature. Uniquely among animals, man was put together from two qualitatively different sorts of matter. The contradictory nature of humans, Rousseau claimed, was caused by the fact that they were made from matter that was "both sentient and insentient"—in other words, from body and soul, body and psyche. "Physical evil," therefore, was inevitable, Rousseau claimed, "in any system of which man was a part."[21]

Rousseau did not actually hold either of the two notions usually attributed to him, namely that originally man's life was good, or that in the subsequent development of the human species our evils outweighed our goods. Goodness was simply the initial harmony between creature and habitat, which was the fate (or good fortune) of all animals. It disappeared from man's grasp because changes in the human habitat did not trigger a corresponding physical adaptation of human instincts. Rather, it triggered mental—that is, moral or social—adaptation. The human trick, as it were, was that mental adaptation could lead to an artificial or social extension of human physical capabilities. Man could not learn to fly like a bird, but he could build airplanes, as we all know by now. In Rousseau's vocabulary, "perfectibility" was the name of this phenomenon.[22] Humans broke out of the animal-like jail of predetermined natural or physical needs. The human mind, the human imagination, created new, artificial needs, which humans then scrambled to satisfy. This was the pulling power to which humans constantly responded in society. The problem was not that humans could only dream or imagine but that they could indeed realize these dreams—not always, not all of them, and not instantly, but over time they could rise to the challenge.

The image of Rousseau as a Cynic, as a Diogenes, suggests that Rousseau was totally against the tricks that the mind can play on the body. Refined or subtle Cynicism, however, was not the minimalist creed of the philosopher in the tub, masturbating in front of the crowd to

21. Jean-Jacques Rousseau, "Letter to Voltaire," in *The Discourses and Other Early Political Writings*, p. 234.

22. Rousseau, "Second Discourse," pp. 148, 159.

relieve his natural or animalistic sexual urges. For Rousseau, man was a developmental or civilizing animal because of the creative tension between his body and his mind. The question was how to exploit this tension without creating a great deal of moral evil. The answer was that the developmental trajectories of mind and body had to be in accord, and the catch-up game between body and mind had to be played delicately. The task was to ensure that the pull of artificial needs and the human ability to satisfy them did not get too far out of sync, or stay out of sync for too long, thereby creating immense tensions and suffering. In Rousseau's words, needs and strength had to grow hand in hand, pari passu, harmoniously.

As Rousseau knew, this rarely happened. Humans developed by leaps and bounds. In the field of political economy, his prime example was precisely the case that I have been discussing here, namely the imbalance in economic development between industry and agriculture. There was nothing wrong or evil with economic development as such. What was wrong, damaging, and morally evil was unbalanced growth: the runaway growth of cities, luxury, and industry, leaving behind a world with weak agriculture, perennial problems with the food supply, often creating deprivation and famine—a demographic and environmental catastrophe. From this perspective, man did not have to return to the forests on all fours and start eating acorns again, as if humans had gone back to being primitive hunter-gatherers. Rousseau was flabbergasted that some of his readers drew this immensely stupid conclusion from reading his work. What he wanted was a society based on labor and personal private property, developing an exchange-based commercial society in which everything grew in a balanced way, where the creative tensions between body and mind were exploited harmoniously, both in man-to-nature and human-to-human, or social, relationships.

This desire for balanced growth was one of the leading ideas in French politics in Rousseau's time. France's rise to greatness under Louis XIV had been achieved at the cost of deliberately knocking the French economy and society off balance. This policy, known as Colbertism, created what was said to be a disaster for France. Recovery from this condition was one of the most widely shared dreams of the eighteenth century. Its prophet was François Fénelon, archbishop of Cambrai and author of the most widely read secular book of the Enlightenment, *The Adventures of Telemachus*. This was the book that Rousseau's characters

Émile and Sophie had to read as the best political moral tale that there was. Fénelon thought that Louis XIV had gone about reviving the ancient Roman project of grandeur and had sought to finance it, with the help of Colbert, by promoting the growth of luxury in France. This resulted most fundamentally in putting unregulated populist *amour-propre* at the center of the French social imagination but also in actively supporting the unbalanced growth of cities, which was taken to be necessary for luxury to thrive. Industry was fostered at the expense of agriculture to generate a huge income for militarism. The central counterexperiment in Telemachus, the state-building experiment of Salentum under the good king Idomeneus, which was to provide the Jacobins in the French Revolution with their economic self-understanding, was a heroic attempt to create a balanced economy. Crucially, it had two stages. The first was to use state power to brutally rebalance both society and the economy through the destruction of cities, expelling the luxury sector's population back to the countryside, abolishing luxury and economic inequality, and, instead of ostentatious display, introducing a symbolic system of ranks as the expression of the natural inequality among men. Mao and Pol Pot in Asia tried to implement plans like this in the twentieth century, but this violent revolutionary experiment of rectifying modern civilization was constantly in the minds of eighteenth-century moralists and economic reformers. They knew how dangerous a vision it was in its original version and continuously looked for more peaceful alternatives, Rousseau and Smith among them. Once the violent correction had happened, the project was not that of primitivism but of balanced growth, in which welfare would constantly be on the rise, but cities would never be allowed to run ahead of the countryside again. In a well-structured economy, free exchange and free trade could reign, and political power could retreat to a distant supervisory role. The orchestra could play, even if it needed a conductor to give it a good tempo, or, to use another metaphor, the well-planned garden could blossom on its own, only occasionally needing a gardener to prune wild growth (these were Fénelon's famous metaphors for a balanced economy). The Physiocrats founded modern economic science on this immensely popular idea.

Rousseau, like many of his Swiss contemporaries, was also a Fénelonian. He wanted a balanced Europe and a libertarian state supervising it. Later, we will see how he imagined such a state working politically and economically, as a republican federation of small republics or cantons based on an equally federally organized network of agriculturally rooted household economies. What we need to discover now, in the remainder of this chapter, is why Smith became the bête noire of this Enlightened Fénelonian crowd, or why he begged to differ.

The issue was not a value choice. There was little on which Rousseau and Smith, as well as many others, would have disagreed. Smith was livid when dogmatic friends of virtue accused him of moral or political betrayal of their pet dreams. Of course a militia was a tolerably good idea for a summer school on civics for teenagers, he maintained, and it might work for insurgencies and the desperate defense of one's homeland, but there was no place for these ragtag armies in modern warfare among economic superpowers. The issue was to work out how to have modern virtue, not its operatic simulacrum on the stage (Rousseau, by the way, agreed with this particular point). Smith didn't simply think that these mistakes were signs of sentimental idiocy, though they were. The mistake was primarily methodological. This was the core idea underlying his growing opposition to natural jurisprudence, which he took to be the foundation of modern economics. In this comparative context, Rousseau is the proper economist—the Physiocrats were shrewd enough to spot this immediately—and Smith the historicist, the cautious and empirical thinker. This takes us back to the territory of the switch back from natural law to Roman law that I described in Chapter 4. Rousseau despaired of history. What he was looking for instead was the equipment to explain large-scale developments, which could then lead to reform, as was laid out so clearly in *The Social Contract* to take only the most obvious example. "History," Rousseau wrote, "in general is defective in that it records only palpable and distinct facts which can be fixed by names, places, and dates." What was needed, he continued, was a way to discover "the slow and progressive causes of these facts, which cannot be similarly assigned." For historians, he lamented, these causes, or the underlying instances of dynamics, "always remain unknown."[23] Rousseau warned his readers that he was perhaps writing historically, insofar as time was a factor in what he was modeling, but he was constructing natural law or theoretical economics. He wanted to know how things develop normally, in the "ordinary course of things." Smith's

23. Rousseau, *Émile*, bk. 4, OC 529, p. 394.

Book III of *The Wealth of Nations*, or his grand answer to all French Fénelonians and addicts of the natural-law idiom, started with a decisive debunking of this methodology. It was certainly true that natural law—the ordinary course of history—and natural progress modeling were logically and even historically correct at a very high level of abstraction. It was certainly true, he added, that "first things first" is the right sequencing of development. One eats first, before one embarks on globalized trade of exotic luxuries. Occasionally this sequence could be perverted, but not systematically and not for long. The fact was, however, that in Europe, the balance of growth was systematically kicked out of kilter and had gone on for centuries. The French Fénelonians were entirely wrong to see Colbertism as a short-term aberration caused by Louis XIV's vainglorious revival of ancient republican monarchism. It was a deliberate policy that had failed to meet its short-term objectives. But the underlying idea was the leitmotif of the entire development of the history of modern Europe. Natural law and its offspring, economics, might have been right about the general development of mankind. They just happened to be wrong about Europe. Modern Europe—not ancient Europe, which had other special features, as we saw in Chapter 4— developed not according to the logic of the natural progress of opulence, the ordinary course of things, but the other way around, or in a retrograde manner, as Smith put it. The sun rising in the East and going down in the West was the ordinary course of things. The sun rising in the West would have created a retrograde movement, and this, to say the least, called for a special explanation. Well, the economic sun of Europe did rise in the West, Smith claimed, and a very special explanation was indeed badly needed. This is what *The Wealth of Nations* was designed to deliver. In this respect, Smith was not a natural jurist and hence not an economist. He was certainly not analytically timid; he just thought that the analytical social philosophers had chosen their target badly. The abstract analytical thinker was Rousseau. His stock is still sky high in the modern analytical philosophy camp, including Oxford, although analytical political thought is now the hallmark of North American republicanism, now known under the misnomer of left-wing liberalism. The United States was meant to be the paradigm case of balanced economic growth, with agriculture first. It turned out to be quite otherwise, and the debate about how this could have happened is still raging on.

Smith thought that Europe's economic development was systematically unbalanced, but he also thought that the balance should be regained
by working with the grain by means of specially tailored policies, rather
than working against it. The key here, again, is in understanding the
discontinuity in Europe's development, the huge gap between the ancients and moderns. In the second *Discourse*, Rousseau drew a picture
of the Roman Republic and then sketched out what needed to be cor-
rected in order to get the political structure of the post-Calvinist Genevan city-state just right. Analytically, he drew a continuous development model of unbalanced economic growth from early human
beginnings to the eighteenth-century French monarchy. Neither of
these continuist-style models was appropriate for modeling what had
happened in Europe. That is why Smith was so adamant that western
or perhaps northern Europeans should break away from their enchant-
ment with local political developments in Tuscany or the lagoon state
of Venice. The apparent neo-ancient development of the Italian, and
later the Swiss, city-states was a sideshow, even if in many ways an in-
structive one. Modern Europe was German, large and rural, and had
started off again with the post-shepherd, not post-ancient, political development of feudalism. What Europe needed was a general transition
to urbanized agricultural-commercial society, not localized instances
of progress in tiny city-state settings. The crux of this matter was speed.
From the perspective of general history, this was bound to happen sooner
or later—mostly later, under the pressure of demographic growth. This
is the same story, in essence, that Rousseau had told about Africa. Development was bound to come, slowly, over tens or perhaps hundreds
of thousands of years. The fast action happened in the North, and this
was mankind's real history, for Rousseau too. He was indignant when
people assumed that he believed that Geneva was a dusty hamlet of evan-
gelical Protestants. It was a prosperous city of watchmakers, he wrote.
(He didn't want it to have a theater, but this was another matter.) He
wasn't completely deluded. Smith, hailing from Kirkcaldy, was also only
interested in the North and realized that more than one catastrophe
had happened there. He badly needed an economic model for the historically ultra-fast transformation of the German shepherds into modern
economic republicans and the temporary masters of the world. How had
they acquired a modern urban-commercial civilization so fast? Where
had it come from, once they had destroyed the flourishing Roman Empire, which once extended as far as Hadrian's wall?

Why did commerce and the cities come up so fast? And what ruined the seemingly impregnable stranglehold of the shepherds on power structures? Smith had to explain the transition problem. He knew that there was no anti-feudal revolution, parliamentary or otherwise. The shepherd societies had collapsed from the inside. The masterstroke of this explanation was that the two events, the rise of commerce and the demise of feudalism, had the same cause. Not proximately, but precisely. I mentioned in Chapter 4 that Smith knew that the economic and legal structure of the cities, but not their politics, had survived. What killed the virtuous military shepherds was the same thing that had devastated their virtuous Greek and Roman predecessors: luxury. For baubles and trinkets they sold their souls and power. A revolution was effected by two kinds of agents, neither of which had any such intention in even the slightest degree. These were the merchants who sold their luxury goods, and the feudal ruling class who took the goods off their hands to satisfy their fancy, tickled by the huge psychological pressure of *amour-propre* that became institutionalized in the honor system. Smith was no friend of luxury, but he insisted that those who did not see that Europe's modern liberty was the child of luxury were blind. If this were so, luxury could not be seen as simply evil or the bane of healthy growth. It was the father, or perhaps the mother, of modern republicanism. I don't think that Rousseau disagreed with the essence of this analysis, at least as far as the destruction of the lords was concerned. The outstanding question was where to go from there. Both Rousseau and Smith knew that the political system that emerged from feudalism was absolutism. They both hated it and wanted to see what was to come of the endgame. The second *Discourse* stated that absolutism, having been built on luxury and inequality in the first place, could not stop it or rectify it. In fact, it made everything much worse, thus sowing the seeds of collapse, anarchy, revolution, and a cyclical or gyratory repetition. Smith saw this possibility and put all his analytical energy into preventing it. Luxury was the foundation of absolutism; it could not be abolished or wished out of existence. But if one understood its workings and how it had destroyed feudalism, one could learn to work with it. To do this, the precise economic logic of the European economy had to be understood properly. Possibly luxury could destroy not only feudal oppression but also absolutist hegemony. Smith thought that a European revolution (a bad thing indeed) could be averted and a new age of legality and economic prosperity could be ushered in, provided imperialism,

nationalism, and the spirit of militarism could be eliminated from
Europe. His agenda was similar to Rousseau's, including a huge shared
emphasis on international affairs. It wasn't that luxury should be destroyed; it simply had to be tamed. This was what Rousseau couldn't
believe. Balanced growth was also Smith's ideal. His means of achieving
it were, however, different. But this topic will be the subject of Chapter 6.

～ 6

Political Economy: Nationalism, Emulation, and War

$\mathcal{T}$HIS CHAPTER REPRESENTS the second installment of the discussion of political economy in a comparative historical perspective. I will leave behind Rousseau's and Smith's histories of mankind and Europe and turn to their discussions of their own age. For both, contemporary politics included issues of the economy and, in close relation to it, the issue of war. Commerce, they observed, did not diminish warfare, as theories of commerce suggested that it would, but increased it. War loomed large in the thought of Rousseau and Smith, whose most productive periods of intellectual creativity coincided with the Seven Years' War. Foreign relations, and especially foreign economic relations, were an essential part of the political thought of their time. Kant's famous essay on perpetual peace published in the age of the French Revolution was in many ways a direct commentary on Rousseau's work on the European peace plan of the abbé de Saint-Pierre, a study that Rousseau had undertaken at the behest of the abbé Gabriel Bonnot de Mably, who himself was the author of a history of diplomacy and the treaty arrangements of modern Europe. Rousseau knew his Montesquieu well, but he had also read his Saint-Pierre attentively. When in his late work, *Considerations on the Government of Poland*, he described the kind of government he advocated, he referred to Saint-Pierre's system of *Polysynodie*, or the experimental plan of a reformed system of government that Saint-Pierre had proposed during the regency that followed the

111

reign of Louis XIV. This was a network of expert councils or government departments operating on a federated basis. It is likely that many of his readers knew what he was referring to and did not think that this type of government was Rousseau's invention. They saw Rousseau as picking his way through the various reform plans of eighteenth-century Europe. Systems not unlike the *Polysynodie* were actually put into place in Prussia and Austria in the 1750s. If we concentrate on these contextual themes, Rousseau appears much less original than he is often made out to be. Conversely, without knowing this context, we simply would not know what his real originality consisted of.

Both Rousseau and Smith, but Rousseau in particular, would be called realists in today's international relations parlance. Rousseau insisted that strong states would always attack weak ones if they could find an opportunity to do so. Conflict and violence were ever present in modern international society. Neither Smith nor Rousseau was a utopian or revolutionary thinker. Both subscribed to the idea of passive obedience and to the sanctity of sovereignty. Rousseau couched his view in a Hobbesian idiom, while Smith referred to Plato's *Crito* and compared revolution to killing one's parents. Both emphasized that revolutions did indeed happen, sometimes frequently, but took them to be simply facts of regime collapse and not as glorious outcomes of rights of resistance.

This is one reason why Rousseau's use of Locke in property theory was somewhat incongruous. Locke, as Bishop Berkeley argued, had written the best book on resistance, while the other side, he thought, was best represented by Plato.[1] Rousseau's reference to Hobbes and Smith's invocation of Plato's *Crito* were easily decipherable by their readers as signals of their respective positions. Both the Genevan and the Scot were theorists of rightful authority—in other words, of the law. This could easily go hand in hand with a realist stance in international affairs. When the Swiss natural philosopher Albrecht von Haller described Rousseau as a modern Carneades, he knew what he was insinuating.[2] Rousseau consistently took the modern world to be swayed solely by the exercise of power and hence to have no moral consistency.

1. George Berkeley, *Passive Obedience; or, The Christian Doctrine of Not Resisting the Supreme Power, Proved and Vindicated* (London: H. Clements, 1712).
2. Albrecht von Haller, *Fabius und Cato, ein Stück der Römischen Geschichte* (Bern and Göttingen: E. Haller, 1774).

In Book III of *The Wealth of Nations*, Smith concluded his history of Europe at the point when modern international power politics came into existence. Feudalism self-destructed due to the erosion of its social and economic base by luxury and as a result of a series of unintended policy mistakes by both kings and nobility. The breakdown of this grotesque political order, which the shepherd polities had superimposed on Europe's Roman foundations, should have produced a peaceful and free modern world, but this sadly was not the case. The suppression of the power of the feudal nobility led to strong central governments or, in other words, to royal absolutism. This change coincided with the military revolution and had two major effects. The first was the emerging dominance of Europe over the rest of the world. This was the age of discoveries, geographical expansion, and the beginnings of Europe's colonial adventures. This, Smith wrote, gave Europe its break (in *The Wealth of Nations*, he paraphrased Raynal's *Philosophical and Political History of the Settlements and Trade of the Europeans in the East and West Indies* when introducing the theme).[3] After the Renaissance, Europe came to form a continental market, roughly the size of the market of China's maritime provinces. This could have been enough to be the basis of decent economic growth, just as it was in China. But because of the discoveries and the superiority of European shipping and military technology, Europe also acquired a huge external market. The result was a spectacular acceleration of economic growth. Globalization had some spectacularly bad consequences, not just economically but also politically. Military power grew fast and, with it, the financial needs of the state. The profitability of commerce raised the specter of intra-European imperialism and the possibility of uniting Europe under the hegemony of a single state. This was the meaning of the idea of universal monarchy (an adaptation of the Roman claim of being lords of the world or the universe to the European theater of state building). Absolutism, the centralized modern monarchy, became the political and administrative vehicle of this ambition.

This type of modern monarchy learned from the economic examples of the Italian city-states (remember that Smith thought that the

3. Guillaume-Thomas François Raynal, *A Philosophical and Political History of the Settlements and Trade of the Europeans in the East and West Indies*, trans. J. Justamond (London: T. Cadell, 1776).

key to understanding Italian republicanism was the fact that Italian city-
states were two hundred years ahead of the large monarchies in economic development). Following the collapse of feudalism Europe became
a hothouse of economic and military competition between states. This
caused, Smith continued his argument, a merger of ideas of economic
and military competition, with very bad consequences. This scheme
of politics was the mercantile system. A state, economically speaking,
was a commonwealth of consumers. The mercantile class, when ad-
vising the state, acted as a representative of the export producers, a small
subset of the nation. The merchants wanted profits and the government wanted a large military budget, so that together they ended up
conspiring against the majority. What enabled them to do so was the
skillful exploitation of inflamed nationalism—or, as Smith called it,
national animosity. A beggar-thy-neighbor type of aggressive economic
foreign policy came into existence. This was what the first Earl of Shaftesbury was already calling jealousy of trade—justified by the national
interest.[4] It was this combination of national animosity and special economic interests masquerading as the national interest that had, Smith
claimed, distorted the politics of modern Europe. He was an enemy of
the mercantile system in every dimension, and the book that followed his
history of the demise of feudalism—that is, Book IV of *The Wealth of
Nations*—was devoted to making a grand attack on this seventeenth- and
eighteenth-century symbiosis of power, commerce, and empire.

Smith showed that mixing the logic of war and trade led to economic
policies that were mistaken and inefficient. He advocated withdrawal
from this poisonous mixture because the continuation of this set of policies was bound in the long run to mortally damage Britain. To better
enable survival, Smith consistently advocated that the state withdraw
from interfering with markets. His famous statement that it was not
enough for the mercantile and financial classes to withdraw from ad-
vising government—that government had to withdraw altogether from
economic intervention, even if it claimed that it was promoting the
common good—came in a more specific context.

This context formed part of Smith's discussion of the reform plans
of the French opposition to the monarchy's policies during the Seven

4. Hont gives Shaftesbury's words, taken from *Delenda Est Carthago*, more accurately
in "Jealousy of Trade: An Introduction" (p. 1): "There is not so Lawful or Commendable a
Jealousie in the World, as an *English Man's*, of the growing Greatness of any Prince or State
at Sea."

Years' War. Like Fénelon in relation to Louis XIV, the Physiocrats—or *economists*, as they were usually called by their contemporaries—set out to present a virtuous alternative to Louis XV's state policy. François Quesnay, Physiocracy's leading light, was a direct moral descendant of Fénelon, with both aiming at a reversal of Colbert's pro-industrial policy. Instead of an emphasis on the cities, agriculture needed to be rebuilt as the foundation of the nation in order to establish a durable framework for balanced growth. I have already talked about Smith's understanding of Europe's retrograde—that is, city-led—pattern of development. Here I want to put the emphasis on another aspect of Smith's critique of corrupt Europe.

Smith argued that in human history, there is never unequivocally healthy development. From this perspective, the medical vision of Quesnay—a very speculative physician, as Smith dubbed him—and its aspiration to cure society of its ills was mistaken and therefore counterproductive. Colbert, Smith argued, had achieved more or less what he wanted, but his opponents and critics, if they ever had the opportunity to get their hands on the rudder of government, would generate perverse results. For Smith, the corrupt masters of mankind were not the sole target that the political reformer had to bear in mind. He also criticized the delusions of those who wanted reform (these were the people whom Germans call *Schwärmer*). If there ever was an Enlightenment project, Smith was its committed enemy. There was, he argued, not sufficient human knowledge available to any government to safely realign Europe's economy according to a preconceived model of balanced growth. History was complex, and national systems of political economy were large. Perfect systems had never existed. If their existence was a genuine precondition of economic and political success, Europe could never have risen to reach its modern condition. "If a nation could not prosper without the enjoyment of perfect liberty and perfect justice," Smith announced in what is arguably one of the most important sentences of *The Wealth of Nations*, "there is not in the world a nation which could ever have prospered."[5] It was important not to act under the influence of theoretical hubris and, even more importantly, not to use the absolute power of the modern state to implement theoretical fantasies. Nothing was more dangerous than the alliance between the theoretical arrogance of the economist-philosophers, the men of

5. Adam Smith, *The Wealth of Nations* (London: T. Nelson and Sons, 1868), IV.ix, p. 280.

ideas, and the political arrogance of government, the men of action. The
great post–Louis XIV French project of righting the balance of the European economy had to be abandoned. "The sovereign," Smith declared,
must be "completely discharged from a duty, in the attempting to perform which he must always be exposed to innumerable delusions, and
for the proper performance of which no human wisdom or knowledge
could ever be sufficient; the duty of superintending the industry of private people, and of directing it towards the employments most suitable
to the interest of the society."[6] The "interest of the society," the last
phrase, refers specifically to the European economic dream of establishing an institutional framework of properly sequenced and balanced
growth, a balance between industry and agriculture.

The proponents of this plan, whose ideas Smith thought were bound
to lead to jeopardy, perversity, and unintended consequences, thought
that it was the absolute duty of the state to provide a framework for economic growth. As I have argued, Rousseau was one of those who thought
that the industry-agriculture imbalance was at the very core of the corruption of France and of modern monarchies in general. Equally clearly,
Jean-Jacques Rousseau was not one of these hubristic reformers. Rousseau could see the point of strong regulatory power, but he thought that
the remedy was worse than the disease. His article on "Political
Economy" in the *Encyclopédie*, an article that its editor, Diderot, took
to be a travesty of the task Rousseau had been asked to perform, began
with the idea that the economy of a state was like a national household,
or *oikonomia*. It was like the traditional family *oikos*, but larger. Households were traditionally governed by fathers or masters, who were responsible for their family and servants, including apprentices. The national household, however, could not have a true collective father or
master, and the impersonation of the role by an elected father was just
the solution that Rousseau categorically rejected. To create a national
father was a solution that was bound to be despotic. Rousseau did wish
to endow the state with powers of interfering with the economy, but
such powers were for rectification only, not for planned reforms. Rousseau wanted a taxation state—that is, using taxation as an instrument
of social engineering, mainly as a bulwark against luxury. I will return
to this point shortly. First, however, I want to show that Rousseau's idea

6. Ibid., IV.ix.51.

of seeing the national household as a confederation of households rather than a scaled-up version of a single household was the functional equivalent of Smith's call for the withdrawal of government from economic management. It is important to realize that the economic face of the confederation was a market between households. Rousseau was not an economic primitivist: the households in question would have economic surpluses that they would trade with one another and also, when appropriate, with other nations. Once a household could produce as much as was enough to meet the needs of two households, it traded. What to produce, how to trade, and so on, had to remain the prerogative of the individual households, because the possibilities and opportunities were best known by their heads. It was their knowledge and behavior that determined the shape of the economy. Their political and moral commitments were a part of their identity. The fathers could manage their domains at this scale, but their knowledge, Rousseau claimed, had no national equivalent. Nor, by extension, was there any need to create a national equivalent (here it becomes abundantly clear why Rousseau in Geneva in the middle of the eighteenth century bothered to refute Sir Robert Filmer).

Rousseau wrote a great deal about economic households. In his most famous novel, *Julie ou la Nouvelle Héloïse*, he gave detailed descriptions of household management by Julie and Wolmar. In his polemical short book against d'Alembert's views on Geneva in the *Encyclopédie*, he described both the society and the economy of the backward Swiss region of the Valais and injected into it an account of his youthful encounter with the mountainside watchmaking communities in the Jura, near Neuchâtel, which was then a Prussian-Swiss city. The region's inhabitants lived on farmsteads with their extended families, not too close but not too far from one another (there was enough society, but not too much, to control *amour-propre*). They had considerable knowledge and curiosity for learning and had reached a very high level of sophistication in artisanal industrial production. They did not subdivide their labor, and they transmitted their technical understanding from generation to generation orally, but they were still in the vanguard of a knowledge-based specialized commercial society. Their products had to be traded, not consumed locally. Rousseau characterized Geneva as more corrupt. It was essentially a community of artisans and bankers. There was a division between the rich and the poor, and the poor lived in the overcrowded—that is, socialized—circumstances of the tenements, just as Rousseau himself had lived as a child. Here, taxation was highly necessary to keep the social balance.

For Rousseau, taxation was the social instrument to achieve balanced growth and to arrest luxury. He knew Montesquieu's ideas on the topic from *The Spirit of Laws* and modified them. He wanted agricultural producers to be exempt from taxes and was also very reluctant to see a sales tax put on food sold at local markets. He was keen on public provisioning in periods of necessity. Like most of his Swiss or his South German contemporaries in Württemberg, Rousseau supported the use of communal grain silos for famine prevention. Adam Smith famously did not, because he assumed that the grain would be stolen or mismanaged in other ways. Rousseau, in Geneva, and Smith, in Scotland, had different social experiences. Rousseau advocated a poll tax on a progressive scale, to tax individuals according to their wealth. All other taxes had to be sales taxes levied on discretionary consumption or the consumption of luxury goods. Here Rousseau literally followed Montesquieu, who argued that luxury grew along an exponential scale.[7] Rousseau agreed with this diagnosis of the multiplier effect and advocated an exponentially progressive consumption tax on luxuries. He realized, however, that some poor people would rather go hungry than live with the shame of visible poverty and would therefore spend money on luxuries to keep up appearances (Smith made a great deal of a similar point). Nonetheless, progressive consumption taxes on luxury goods (please note, *not* sumptuary laws) were an essential part of his vision of a good state. The general will was there to control rampant inequality, but taxation was also employed to help the general will in both its general and its day-to-day operation. For remaining tax needs, which covered practically all the positive needs of the state, Rousseau advocated taxation in kind, through the supply of goods and also labor, by introducing a national corvée system. The idea here was to cut out the monetization of citizens' contributions to the national household and avoid paying public sector wages to that part of the population involved in directly serving communal needs. Smith warned his English and Scottish contemporaries that taxation in kind was a characteristic of the feudal era, before the monetization of the economy, and had been abolished once the

7. Montesquieu, *The Spirit of the Laws*, pt. 1, bk. 7, chap. 1.

upper classes introduced monetized taxation to support their luxury consumption. Rousseau was not describing a rapacious feudal agricultural economy but a progressive Swiss state, and he had no hesitation in recommending the reintroduction of pre-monetization taxation practices, because they were superior in their manageability to money taxes. National labor service was also meant to be a vehicle of patriotic education, supplementing the militia. Later he recommended the same methods for Poland, not just because parts of Poland had no monetized economy but also to prevent its rise. In Poland there were feudal lords, serfdom, corvée, and no Swiss work ethic. Here, faced with the issue of abolishing Polish feudalism and its economic and social backwardness, Rousseau was out of his depth.

Since liberated serfs had to become good citizens and diligent contributors to the republic, Rousseau suggested establishing a prize competition for good behavior and hard work among Polish serfs. The prize for developing this work ethic would be liberation. The serfs would have to be on their best behavior for a long time to deserve their freedom, thus ensuring that emancipation would occur at a slow and gradual pace. Slowly, serfdom in Poland would disappear, and the population would acquire a culture that despised luxury and prized hard work. Liberalization through monetization, fueled by luxury through a series of unintended consequences, which, according to Smith, had been the past pattern of European development, was something Rousseau wanted to avoid at all costs.

He devised a program of reform involving the participation of the Polish nobility, which was designed to prevent the emergence of a deeply disaffected post-liberation underclass. Rousseau's aim was not to produce a Poland that was a poor primitive backwater in order to avoid the ravages of capitalism: the unregulated reign of dizzy *amour-propre* and the pursuit of luxury, effectively turning Poland into yet another corrupt competitor in the European power game, as Russia was clearly trying to be. He thought that the saved Polish republic should be an active and thriving place, with each citizen (not only the serfs earning their liberation) working hard and performing his or her duty. There was to be a strong Polish economy, whose aim was national self-subsistence. The motivating force underlying social and political life had to be *amour-propre* in all its aspects, producing knowledge, innovation, productive effort, and great consumption; but in each case, the motivating force had to be the healthy variety in which capability and wants, knowledge and desire, grew hand in hand. Only a luxury-loving French *philosophe*, Rousseau wrote, would think that a Rousseauian society was meant to resemble a band of enthusiasts, hell-bent on creating a secular monastery of citizens who lived like ascetic mendicant friars. In the book on Poland, more than anywhere else, it becomes clear what Rousseau's alternative to Montesquieu's monarchy was. He too relied on the composite nature of *amour-propre* and produced a model in which one kind of selfishness was counterbalanced by another. In Rousseau's case, however, the countervailing quest for distinction was based not on false but on true honor. Here he did not have the valor of the battlefield in mind. Rather, he placed the emphasis on a competitive quest for economic and civil distinction. Following the logic of his institutional design, this could not turn into a quest for false honor because it could not be monetized and bought, meaning that it could not turn into a species of luxury. Economically, for Rousseau, as for Locke and many other theorists whom Rousseau had read, money was the key to the dangerous combination of *amour-propre* and inequality. Rousseau's concept of honor was connected to true and useful achievement in competition of effort or industry. This kind of competitive search for distinction was what he called emulation. Here he followed Fénelon, who thought that a corrupt state could never return to true equality and made provision in Salentum for a meritocracy, a system of ranks based on talent and service, which was made highly visible through a dress code. Similarly, Rousseau wanted Poland to be a stratified, articulated, and well-organized society of honor. He designed for the Poles a full panoply of competitions, exercises, uniforms, and decorative badges of merit. In Rousseau's virtuous Polish economy, civic achievements were rewarded with badges of honor, the badges being made of different metals and carrying inscriptions that indicated a person's rank in a meritocratic hierarchy. The goal of this system was to turn the psychological energy of emulation into a source of national technological and agronomic improvement. Societies for improvement were expected to organize regular competitions to reinforce citizens' desire to make healthy progress in pursuit of honor. The aim of the republic was not virtuous poverty but an honest, good life for all based on honest work by all. Consumption could grow, but it would be spread evenly among the citizenry and would be taxed vigilantly to prevent inequality from entering the system through the back door. In some of his other writings, Rousseau showed his interest in the pitfalls of even the most virtuous policy of economic improvement. Like Montesquieu, he disliked machines. He recognized, for example, the benefits of a more efficient way of drawing a plow than a pair of oxen, but he also worried that fewer oxen would mean that less cheap meat would be available for the consumption of the urban poor, a shortfall in the meat supply that needed to be offset by a healthy vegetarian and lactose-rich diet.

This was the kind of civil society that could undergird a healthy state. People formed by this culture would constitute the human material of a general will. Poland, however, was not a city-state like Geneva. The Polish republic had to be both monarchical and representative. The civil society of emulative and honor-bound agricultural improvement societies could ensure that the election of representatives was not corrupt. Meritocratic knights of turnip production also made the best material for rising up the political ranks, nominated by their patriotic local improvement societies. They would provide the pool of candidates for election through gradual promotion from step to step through each meritocratic rank. The lack of any hierarchy in society, Rousseau thought, was likely to create rhapsodies of self-promotion within the luxurious imaginations of status seekers. The human mind needed order and imagination and had to be cooled down to operate in a controlled and disciplined fashion. In a republic based on work, where the market directly connected producers and consumers, honor achieved in work was just the right foundation for a political career. For Rousseau, sovereignty could not be represented in a Hobbesian sense, but a pyramid of representatives could still be built to encompass a large and populous country (the two concepts of representation were not identical—Rousseau's, like Hume's ideal commonwealth for England, was designed on quasi-Harringtonian lines). A large republic had to be a federation of little local republics, and the national diet based on local assemblies. As with the idea that the government, not the legislative body or sovereign, should be a *Polysynodie*, so too was the interest in dietines or analogous local units a standard idea of European political discourse.

There are very few original ideas in Rousseau's plan for Poland. It rather confirmed the suspicion of his contemporaries that he had been working with the same pool of political ideas as everyone else. What was noticeable was that he kept his design under better control than others and was unusually coherent in the detailed implementation of his purpose: the healthy market economy driven by honor-oriented labor

and innovation issued in a federal polity whose sovereignty was not represented and whose government was based on a coherent system of the
separation of powers. Two points were very noticeable in this plan. One
was Rousseau's acute awareness of objections to the problem of a weak
executive body and attendant problems of semi-anarchy in decision
making. He strove to design effective government. Second, his aim was
to avoid England's mistakes. A corrupt legislative body was the fate of
England, which of course was something that Rousseau knew from
Montesquieu. Therefore, he wanted frequent parliaments and imperative mandates. Since the sovereign assembly had no other task but to
decide about principles, inflexible imperative mandates could work perfectly well. The diet needed no flexible prerogative or loosely defined
executive powers: these were a matter for government alone. These ideas,
Rousseau claimed, were identical to the principles he had set out in *The
Social Contract*. Those who are surprised by this might profitably reread
their *Social Contract* and do so more carefully than the first time, just
as the abbé Sieyès and many of his contemporaries did in the generation after Rousseau, when they could read the Poland book and the *Essay
on the Origin of Languages* in the posthumous volumes of Rousseau's collected works that were published soon after his death. These thinkers
were certainly followers of Rousseau, but not of the Rousseau depicted
in later literature as a small state virtue fantasist who aspired to be the
modern Diogenes and dreamed about a return to the natural goodness
of physical man. It is enough to read Rousseau's commendation of the
spirit of innovation driving the worthies of rural improvement societies
in hot pursuit of the bronze or silver badges that signaled that their
owners were champion beekeepers or master watchmakers or, for that
matter, captains of the local militia or superintendents of a charity or
school (or, alternatively, his fascination with Swiss watchmaking technology) to realize the deeply eighteenth-century and Swiss vision of the
world that Rousseau was projecting. He liked the Swiss hero of the story
about the rural Socrates, Kleinjogg, who was an innovative champion
farmer.[8] Not a gentleman as in England, Scotland, or Ireland, but a
peasant farmer who was a Socratic citizen and upholder of the general

8. Hans Caspar Hirzel, *Die Wirtschaft eines Philosophischen Bauers*, originally published
in Volume 1 of the *Abhandlungen der Naturforschenden Gesellschaft in Zürich* (Zurich:
Heidegger und Comp., 1761). A French edition appeared the following year under the title
Le Socrate rustique, ou description de la conduite économique et morale d'un paysan philosophe
(Zurich: Heidegguer, 1762).

will. This was the real road to wealth and virtue, not imitation of the metropolitan economies of the crowded, unhealthy, and luxurious capital cities of the large European states, with their false glitter and seemingly easy social mobility. Rousseau desperately wanted to rein in comparative envy and the desire for national grandeur that fueled these sorts of arrangements. Healthy nations needed an equally competitive but hearty rather than diseased *amour-propre*.

I now want to turn back to Smith. The most appropriate comparative angle is provided, I think, by his theory of foreign trade. We are all accustomed to seeing Smith as a sworn enemy of mercantilism or the idea that societies must get rich on trade. Instead, it is usually also argued, and in the same vein, that Smith concentrated on production. This might be true, but one also needs to ask the question: Production for which markets? Domestic markets alone, or also for foreign or world markets? It is important to realize that Smith was a real enthusiast of the export trade, or production for consumers in other nations. He thought hard and deep about international economic competition and about strategies for achieving, maintaining, and—if possible— perpetuating export competitiveness. Smith would have been a mercantilist had he agreed on the use of national military and political power to achieve this aim, but he resolutely rejected this option and was very surprised that, despite his violent attack on English policy, he received such a favorable response in Parliament. He was probably the first to suspect that *The Wealth of Nations* had not really been read properly. To take one prominent example, Smith was against using the colonial system to prop up national exports. This was an evasion of competitiveness rather than its consummation. It was easy to saturate captive markets, but this was a recipe for decline. A country selling shoddy products forcibly to its own underlings would inevitably grow lazy and inefficient. Tough competitors who had to fight for their markets would sooner or later overtake Britain, and the once proud imperial and industrial power would then fall back to where it belonged, to the position of a middle-sized European nation that had fallen behind in international economic competition as a consequence of its previous imperial folly. In this prediction, Smith has been proved to be exactly right.

Instead of the ruinous policy of empire, Smith projected a theory of international emulation for Britain. Rousseau's federated market of households and honor-hungry improvement societies represented a domestic model of the economy, faithfully mirroring his national

framework for politics. International competition for honors was un-
derstandable for Rousseau, but it was far too dangerous. It was bound
to be the source of inflamed and uncontrollable national *amour-propre*.
Rousseau's notion of emulation was for home consumption. Smith
tried to extend it to the international arena and, in doing so, came very
close to being completely misunderstood. In fact, we know that his
work was to become the *locus classicus* for the imperialism of free trade.
Nonetheless, it is important to specify that he did not advocate international competition but rather international emulation. We will have
to look at the construction of this theorem as a classic case of producing good economic nationalism (perhaps good economic interna-
tionalism would be a better label) or as an instance of constructive and
progressive national *amour-propre:* of competition without national
animosity, based on the love of mankind. This idiom remains relatively unknown because it is to be found only in the final additions to
The Theory of Moral Sentiments in 1789 rather than in the more famous
Wealth of Nations and was part of Smith's analysis of the practical ethics
of patriotism, not his earlier analysis of international trade. But before
one can see this clearly, one must first understand why this was not an
optional element of Smith's system.

Rousseau was not against benign foreign trade, but he was prepared
to abandon it if it became morally poisonous or competitively difficult.
He wanted vigorous home markets and national self-sufficiency in sta-
ples. Foreign trade was in luxuries, and those could be abandoned without
real loss. Rousseau was fundamentally a closed commercial state theorist, which meant that he rejected the notion that a state had to grow
externally, either through arms or through trade. His idea of balanced
growth was domestic growth based on the sacred right of property,
which everybody had in his or her own labor.

Smith frowned on anyone who questioned his patriotism and devo-
tion to virtue. But foreign trade for him was a key element of the retrograde path that Europe had taken to modernity. He also had to deal
with the fallout of the financial revolution. As Europe's trade grew, its
needs for money, practical specie, grew too. To solve material short-
ages and inconvenience, paper money had to be introduced. Smith hailed
this move as a real innovation, but recognized too that the military-
commercial complex of the modern eighteenth-century state had hi-
jacked this new monetary device for its own purposes. This was the famous issue of public debt, an innovative way to finance warfare that was

first introduced in Renaissance Italy and then in the Dutch Republic. From the end of the seventeenth century, it became the favored instrument of war finance for power-hungry European monarchies, as the political features of early modern republics were borrowed one by one by larger states. Hume was so worried about the betrayal of intergenerational justice housed by public debt (it was a potentially reckless advance expenditure of future tax revenue, or, as Hume put it, drawing bills on posterity) that he advocated voluntary state bankruptcy to get rid of it.[9] The more republican a state became, the more difficult it was to get rid of the debt, because the loans to the state mostly came from its own citizens, whose interest and property the state was supposed to protect. Hume wanted the French monarchy to declare bankruptcy, and at one point in the 1760s, he hoped for the future cardinal Loménie de Brienne to become the French prime minister because he was rumored to favor a voluntary royal bankruptcy. The one great advantage of absolute royal sovereignty was its relative freedom to override the property rights of its subjects. Hume hoped that this power would be used, for once, for a sensible purpose. Smith also thought that the debt would eventually kill any country that adopted it as a regular practice, but for him, Hume's plan was completely unrealistic and dangerous. The right alternative was a sensible foreign policy, here meaning the preservation of Britain as a blue-water power secured by the Navigation Acts (which Smith thought were measures of real republican genius and had been England's salvation) in conjunction with non-intervention in foreign land wars, while still acting as an offshore adjudicator of Europe's balance of power. Smith thought that these two activities could be financed from the profits of foreign trade, tapping into mercantile profits and using emergency powers if war made it necessary. This idea assumed, of course, that international trade took place in the great mercantile republic of mankind under rules of neutrality, allowing commerce to continue even during war. It also implied that the paper instruments that the Treasury received from merchants in times of emergency could be converted into gold and silver cash by the bankers of the great mercantile commonwealth of the world.[10] Somebody, somewhere, would always

9. David Hume, "Of Public Credit," in *Essays Moral, Political and Literary*, ed. E. F. Miller (Indianapolis: Liberty Classics, 1985), p. 361.

10. A similar idea was put forward by Montesquieu, *The Spirit of Laws* (London: J. Nourse, 1750), XX.23 "Riches consist either in lands, or in moveable effects. The soil of every country is commonly possessed by the natives. The laws of most states render

want to buy British bills of exchange for cash. It assumed too that it was possible to tap into the collective gold reserve of the world at relatively short notice. War, as Smith well knew, could not be financed by paper money alone because the value of a paper currency was dependent on the opinion of the people about a country's chances of winning or losing the contest. Finally, assumptions about abundant merchant profits presupposed that the country had export products that were highly competitive, easily transportable, and in demand worldwide. At the time that Smith wrote this policy recommendation, Britain did have this type of trade—the button and toy manufactory based in the Midlands, exploiting both machines and the technical division of labor at the workshop level. It produced cheap, relatively uniform, but high-quality products that were eminently transportable, had relatively little competition, and were sought after by consumers in many countries. Without this type of export capacity, there would have been no national income to pay for Britain's defense and still less for winding down the public debt. Smith would then have ended up where Hume, Rousseau, Kant, and the rest ended up, dreaming about bankruptcy or perpetual peace. Smith did not believe in any of this, nor, as a matter of fact, did Rousseau, Hume, or Kant (but that is another story).

Another alternative was to introduce a closed commercial state, as the Scots Jacobite Sir James Steuart had advocated, or, a little bit later, the German philosopher Fichte.[11] Rousseau advocated it for Poland, Corsica, and Switzerland, but made no suggestion about its possible introduction in France or England. They were a lost cause, and this, in a real sense, was what lay behind Rousseau's prediction of cyclical revolutions in France over the social question and war about imperial and market policy. Smith too toyed with the idea of closed states when writing about the stationary state, but this is too complex an issue to discuss here.

---

foreigners unwilling to purchase their lands; and nothing but the presence of the owner improves them. This kind of riches therefore belongs to every state in particular. But moveable effects, as money, notes, bills of exchange, stocks in companies, vessels, and, in fine, all merchandises, belong to the whole world in general; which, in this respect, is composed of but one single state, of which all the societies upon earth are members."

11. Sir James Steuart, *An Inquiry into the Principles of Political Economy* (London: Printed for A. Millar and T. Cadell in the Strand, 1767); Johann Gottlieb Fichte, *Der geschlossene Handelsstaat: Ein philosophischer Entwurf als Anhang zur Rechtslehre und Probe einer künftig zu liefernden Politik* (Tübingen: Cotta, 1800).

Instead, his export strategy required an open commercial state, which was able to win markets on the merit of its products. The price element of the competition was crucial here. To keep markets, one had to offer products at competitive prices. Prices, it was believed, were mainly determined by wages. High wages were an indication of national happiness and relative equality in a nation. But high wages also implied an inevitable loss of competitiveness. This was where the specter of the impossibility of lasting economic greatness loomed into view, just as it also became a commonplace to deny the very possibility of lasting military or imperial greatness. Smith believed that the solution lay in high productivity, enhanced by the use of machinery and the reorganization of the labor process. Wages could remain high if they were offset by the growth of productivity. There could be a huge number of products emanating from the factory, each being cheap and of a high uniform standard, while the aggregate profit and wages could remain high. To Smith's mind, this solution dispelled the fear that low-wage countries could compete successfully with advanced ones just because their poverty would keep their wage and price levels low and, by doing so, provide them with instant competitiveness. Rousseau still clung to the myth of the military superiority of hardy poor nations over effeminate and luxurious ones, which was a straightforward derivation from the idea that it was luxury that had led to the decline of Rome and its obliteration by the invading German tribal armies. But the new threat was that luxurious nations could lose their export trade when encountering competition from poorer and leaner nations. *The Wealth of Nations* offered a refutation of these ideas. That is why it starts with an emphasis on machines and the technical division of labor, praising productivity as the key to modern economic success in the international arena.

Britain was a composite state, with one rich and three poor national components: Wales, Scotland, and Ireland. The Irish were the first to make a national credo of the belief that they were capable of competing with the English. The English believed them, and the English state clamped down on the Irish economy so brutally that this frightened the Scots into voluntarily entering into a common market with England in the Union of 1707. The Scots first tried to adopt the Dutch model of the entrepôt trade, choosing for this experiment the location of what is today the Panama Canal. It failed both politically and economically, and because it crossed the interests of both England and Spain. The outcome was the formation of the world's first consensual free-trade area, the union between England and Scotland in 1707.

If the mercantile system as Smith presented it was a zero-sum game, it is not obvious that free trade is its opposite. Smith's position on the difficulties involved in the subject is a good case in point. A generation or two later, Friedrich List was to argue that Smith was thinking too much within the framework of Anglo-Scottish-Irish-American trade to fully understand the nature of trade between independent states.[12] Maybe. In any case, Smith already had to contend with the fact that his best and most respected friend in Scotland, David Hume, had applied the Irish logic of trade between rich and poor countries to the subject of Anglo-Scottish trade and had asserted that a sequential transfer or product cycle between rich and poor nations could occur, with simpler and more wage-sensitive industries moving to poor countries, while complex and high value-added products continued to propel rich countries to further greatness. Hume was irked by the slow pace of the working of the Anglo-Scottish economic union and expected this logic to start to operate more forcefully. Many understood him to be prophesying Britain's decline, overlooking the fact that Scotland was as much within Britain as was England. Hume in fact was developing a big argument about the greatest fear of the eighteenth century, and perhaps the next two centuries too—namely the idea of a world trade monopoly. The idea was that rich nations get richer and poor ones poorer, a logic that was close to Rousseau's heart in every way. For Hume, this production transfer mechanism through competition was the solvent of this problem, as it was for its Irish originators.[13]

The idea was presented prominently by Montesquieu in his unpublished essay on universal monarchy as the basis of a future European Union or European peace, because for him, as for many of his French contemporaries, it implied that the English world hegemony in commerce would abate automatically.[14] He put this theory, which he prob-

12. Friedrich List, *The Natural System of Political Economy*, ed. W. O. Henderson (London: Cass, 1983), p. 319. Hont discusses List in "Jealousy of Trade: An Introduction," pp. 148–55.

13. On this see Hont, "The 'Rich-Country-Poor-Country' Debate in the Scottish Enlightenment," in *Jealousy of Trade*; "The 'Rich Country-Poor Country' Debate Revisited: The Irish Origins and the French Reception of the Hume Paradox," in *David Hume's Political Economy*, ed. M. Schabas and C. Wennerlind (Abingdon: Routledge, 2008).

14. Montesquieu, *Réflexions sur la monarchie universelle (1734)*, in *Œuvres Complètes* II, ed. Roger Caillois (Paris: Gallimard, 1951), pp. 19–38.

ably derived from Richard Cantillon, the Irish banker, or from his contacts with the Bolingbroke circle, into the second edition of his book on Rome, republished, as has been mentioned, in 1748 with *The Spirit of Laws*, but he had to censor himself the second time, omitting this dangerous doctrine. The French had many takes on the story. Mably—who put Rousseau on the trail of the abbé de Saint-Pierre and who was seen as the major European theorist of republican political economy—thought that this would cause a disastrously cyclical growth of the European national economies, creating a constant revolutionary danger. Others, like Condillac, Mably's brother, saw the aspect of providential justice in Hume's idea. This was not a mechanism for the rich to lose their status but for the poor to join in—thus, a having the cake and eating it too state of affairs—provided that the rich nations, seeing the writing on the wall, mended their ways and constantly moved toward ever more complex and sophisticated production, preserving their advantage but letting others grow as well, eventually closing the gap between poor and rich nations. Despite this, Condillac also came out on the side of the closed commercial state theorists. Complementary trade, as in exchanging the products of the North and South with one another—that is, trade based on natural endowment heterogeneity or on highly localized nodes of supreme expertise—was all right, but directly competitive trade in the same products, based on wage level differentials and price wars in the home markets of competitor nations, had to be shut down because it was bound to disturb the peace of the world too much, causing war and anarchy. The competitively fueled flux was too difficult to handle without a world state overseeing it. None of these thinkers thought that such a monstrous entity was either feasible or desirable. (There were odd exceptions, like Anacharsis Cloots during the French Revolution, who dreamed of a world *Polysynodie* that would form a political world republic as a counterpart to the global commonwealth of commerce that Montesquieu and Smith had commented on. Cloots duly paid with his head at the hands of Robespierre for suggesting such a dangerous competitor to the Jacobin idea of a semi-closed price-control state.)

Smith knew that his ideas about competitive exporting states had to be decoupled from mercantilist notions of competition. He had to deal with the issue of national animosity, the negative version of national *amour-propre*. This required an appropriately benevolent agency that could lead to the same positive economic outcome. Rousseau was a

philosopher of patriotism par excellence. Emulation was for him a patriotic phenomenon. Smith understood that patriotism was a double-edged
sword. It was far more than vigilance about national security and en-
thusiasm about fulfilling domestic political obligations. "Love of
country" was a psychological phenomenon and had to do with the identity and self-respect of nations and their quest for recognition. Patriots
worshipped the history and culture of their nation, often excessively.
Patriotism was collective pride, whose function was to mitigate individual insecurity. When "we compare [our country] with other societies
of the same kind," Smith wrote, "we are proud of its superiority, and
mortified in some degree, if it appears in any respect below them."
This was the same view as Rousseau's. The economic dimension was
prominent in this view. The "prosperity and glory" of our country, Smith
explained, "seem to reflect some sort of honour upon ourselves."[15] Economic patriotism often came close to the politics of envy. "The love of
our own nation," Smith continued, "often disposes us to view, with the
most malignant jealousy and envy, the prosperity and aggrandisement
of any other neighbouring nation."[16] But without confidence, nations
declined; and without competition, markets were dysfunctional. Hence,
Smith searched for an alternative that maximized both national pride
and economic growth, while eliminating the detrimental consequences
of national prejudice and envy. His alternative was "national emulation,"
the competitive pursuit of national economic excellence for honor. In
classical thought, emulation was the positive version of envy. Emulation was an "anxious desire that we ourselves should excel," and it was
"originally founded in our admiration of the excellence of others."[17]
Envy and emulation were structured similarly, and it was often difficult to separate the two, except that in emulation you wanted to win by
outdoing others, while envy suggested that hindering them would
achieve the same result. The difference, in other words, was in the means
proposed to achieve superiority. In the case of envy, the end justified
any means, just like reason of state. Emulation was also a kind of jealousy. Aristotle's original Greek for the Latin *aemulatio* was *zelos*, or
"zeal," and this was the root of the English word "jealousy" (originally

15. Smith, *TMS*, VI.ii.2.2.
16. Ibid., *TMS*, IV.ii.2.3.
17. Ibid., *TMS*, III.2.3.

"zealousy"). Envy created hatred, and emulation produced zeal, striving, activity, and progress. Emulation did not imply aiming directly at virtue. Rather, it was a child of ambition, a tireless zeal to obtain glory and honor. It was a vehicle for national preeminence. It was the constructive version of *amour-propre*, part of the activity of the comparative national self. For individuals "to deserve, to acquire and to enjoy the respect and admiration of mankind," Smith wrote, "are the great objects of . . . emulation."[18] The same applied to nations. He supported Rousseau's domestic notion of emulation. "Premiums given by the publick to artists and manufacturers who excel in their particular occupations" represented a fair way to promote improvement.[19] Providing nonmarket incentives to emulation in skill and quality could increase technological development and enhance market competition, helping poor countries catch up with richer ones, and creating markets where none existed before.

He applied this notion on a much larger scale, on the national level. In this setting, by definition, emulation had to be a competitor to patriotism. Here, Smith's best suggestion was to temper the national animosity of patriotism with the love of mankind, using the cosmopolitan evaluation of the cultural and economic achievements of other nations as the counterforce to envy. This was highly problematic. National animosity was founded "in pride and resentment."[20] The love of mankind came from a different psychological root and was no match for such passions. The problem with the "love of our own country" was not merely that it was a passion separate from "the love of mankind," constantly requiring individuals and nations to negotiate between their conflicting feelings of love. "Love of mankind," Smith admitted, was the loser in the contest, because "love of country" was by far the stronger sentiment. Worse, Smith claimed, patriotism urged nations "to act inconsistently" with the love of mankind.[21] Both honor and envy were sentiments anchored in comparative assessments of individuals and nations. Honor could incite emulation but could not restrain it from running to excess.

---

18. Ibid., *TMS*, I.iii.3.2.
19. Smith, *WN*, IV.v.a.39.
20. Smith, *TMS*, VI.ii.1.4
21. Smith, *TMS*, VI.ii.2.4.

We have ended up at an interesting place. This is the territory of the first two chapters of the so-called Geneva manuscript of Rousseau's *Social Contract*, which was a part of his great work on political institutions. The chapter focused on the tension between global and national societies and their attendant social psychologies. Rousseau dropped it from the published version of *The Social Contract*, which argued the case solely for national societies. Smith brought it back in *The Theory of Moral Sentiments* to explain patriotism properly. His conclusion was tentative and hesitant. His *Wealth of Nations* talked only about the wealth of nations, not of mankind, which was best achieved, he thought, through a multiplicity of national agencies and not directly. It is quite convenient to finish on a note of failure by both Rousseau and Smith on this issue. The aim is to show that they failed at the same place, and their arguments are often more similar than we tend to assume. Further, it is not clear whether we have gotten that much further. This year, I hope that I will be forgiven more easily for being a bit skeptical about our theoretical progress. This is a good time to start thinking again by reconsidering the apparently opposite systems of Rousseau and Smith. We cannot but learn from the comparison. *Amour-propre*, the nation-state, and commerce are still the bread and butter of modern political theory, while *The Wealth of Nations* and *The Social Contract* are still among the most frequently mentioned books of modernity. This book will have achieved its aim if it has given you some reason to see why they remain so, but with a different reading than has hitherto been the case. The misunderstandings of these great texts have gone on far too long.

Index

133